PERSUASIVE WRITING

PERSUASIVE WRITING

A Manager's Guide to Effective Letters and Reports

Patricia C. Weaver
Robert G. Weaver

THE FREE PRESS
A Division of Macmillan Publishing Co., Inc.
NEW YORK

Collier Macmillan Publishers
LONDON

The Free Press
A Division of Macmillan Publishing Co., Inc.
866 Third Avenue, New York, N.Y. 10022

Collier Macmillan Canada, Ltd.

Library of Congress Catalog Card Number: 76-7178

Printed in the United States of America

printing number

2 3 4 5 6 7 8 9 10

Library of Congress Cataloging in Publication Data

Weaver, Patricia C
    Persuasive writing.

    Bibliography: p.
    Includes index.
    1. Commercial correspondence. 2. Business
report writing. I. Weaver, Robert G., joint
author. II. Title.
HF5721.W33 1976   651.7'4   76-7178
ISBN 0-02-934020-9

Contents

Part Three

HOW TO USE THE TOOLS OF THE WRITING CRAFT

List of Exhibits

Preface

This handbook is intended to help you do the writing your job demands. If you are the proprietor of a small business or a manager at any level in an industry, a military organization, government agency, church, school, labor union, or any other enterprise, you must write letters, memos, and reports. Whether you want to or not you must write to explain things, to smooth relationships, to convince others of the value of some course of action. Such writing must be clear, concise, complete, and correct. It must convey your message with businesslike good humor in a courteous tone. Our handbook identifies the range of this kind of writing, the forms it takes, and the expository and persuasive techniques it requires.

We have sought first of all to comfort those who feel handicapped in the use of the written language. Many writers in management positions are defeated by the attitude that writing is an awesome craft or perhaps a gift beyond the skill of ordinary mortals. These people do not trust themselves with the language. They go to the files to see what turns of phrase have worked in the past. To overcome their insecurity, they try to write to impress. They hunt the big word to sound erudite. They pad the report to indicate thoroughness. Their writing becomes overly qualified and overly precise, and finally unintelligible.

Our aim is to teach the habits of good writing. With the proper attitude, a respect for how words work together, and knowledge of the conventions of usage, writing can be clear and often graceful. We urge you to trust yourself. Find out what you think, and say what you mean in the simple language you would use with a friend. Make adjustments in your wording until you are sure you are saying what you want to say. Find your voice. Don't be so worried about criticism that you become afraid to write. When you get stuck, look at our table of contents. Chances are your problem will be identified in one of the "how to" sections. Read the appropriate parts for encouragement and practical advice.

We have also addressed another faulty attitude, one that few would admit having because it is often held unconsciously. It is characterized by a lack of respect for the integrity of language, a smug confidence that shoddy ideas can be salvaged by glib locutions, packaged in glistening words, and sold as good ideas. This view holds that you can have your way with people if you learn the art of word manipulation.

We believe that a person in a management position is valuable because he or she has a unique view of reality. When asked to report that view, he must strive to do so with fresh, not borrowed, insight. Then he must have the courage to state clearly the truth he sees. If he can not or will not do that, he is worse than useless because he will give the impression all is well when he knows it is not. Check your drafts for signs of foggy writing. Did you write to impress? To conform? To hide a truth? To avoid responsibility? To hide the fact that there is no idea?

Cloudy writing usually comes when you don't know what you want to say or how to say it. We have tried to identify all those times and have tried to address them in the many "how to" sections of the book.

    How to say no to a customer without losing his goodwill
    How to prepare a summary
    How to use other people's writing

Our handbook covers dozens of practical problems like these, as well as problems of format, style, usage, and other conventions that often plague those responsible for preparing the writing of others.

    How to space a letter on a page
    How to break words
    How to know whether to put question marks inside or outside
        quotation marks

We have made a special effort to focus on those sometimes ambiguous, sensitive areas where errors might confuse, irritate, or mislead a reader, and thereby discredit the boss or the company. In all our "how to" sections we have tried to present the information and advice you will need clearly and with good humor.

We believe our book will help you become a better, more confident writer. If it does, you will become more effective in your job. Because you can transmit your views with precision, economy, courage, and maybe some flair, your world becomes a little safer for you. And that should happen to everybody.

We are indebted to Joseph Anderson, Vicepresident, Public Relations, Dictaphone Corporation; Lorna Daniells at the Baker Library, Harvard University; Carmen Clark at the United States Army War College; and Christian K. Arnold, Associate Director, National Association of State Universities and Land Grant Colleges, for their help with gathering and preparing information for this book.

Throughout this book, we consistently recommend that you show your preliminary drafts to others. If you find a person with the talent, creativity, and patience to help you say precisely what you mean, you are lucky indeed. And that is how we feel—very lucky—to have been assigned Claude Conyers as editorial supervisor of our book. His imaginative suggestions, instructive analysis, and unflagging attention to the details of the manuscript have not only inspired us but have also resulted in a book more consistently helpful to our readers.

Part One

HOW TO WRITE
BUSINESS LETTERS

How to Analyze Your Letter Writing

Let's face it. You wish you didn't have to write business letters at all. And you can find a lot of good reasons to support your contention that you shouldn't have to: letters are expensive; the telephone is more "personal"; mail service is slow and unpredictable; your time is valuable. So you use the telephone whenever possible. You delegate much of the letter writing and make liberal use of form letters. Nonetheless, there still seem to be too many letters you *must* write (you have them on your desk right now) and many more you *should* write. You're even a little nervous about how the letters you have delegated are being handled. And what about those form letters? Are they doing the job? Could the tone be improved? Are they kept current and appropriate to the situations that inspired them? Annoying though the thought may be, you have to write letters, and you would like to be able to do it well enough to feel confident when supervising the writing efforts of subordinates.

The solution to this dilemma is to learn what business letter writing involves and how to do it quickly and correctly.

The business letter is, first, a form of communication, and thus its message must be understood by the reader. Second, it is a representation of you, or your department, or your company and therefore must be courteous and reasoned. *Clarity* and proper *tone,* then, are the two indispensable ingredients of a successful business letter.

To be understood, the letter must be clear. Perhaps the best way to see how to be clear is to examine how and why writing gets unclear.

Somewhere along the way someone told you that letters should sound "natural." "Write like you talk," you were told. While an unstrained, personal tone is certainly desirable and effective, the trouble starts when you begin writing as if you were talking. We have all read the verbatim quotes of famous people—usually presidents and statesmen—and chuckled over the unfinished, rambling thoughts, non sequiturs, and abrupt leaps from one subject to another. The same

3

passage may have been quite clear had we heard the words delivered. Writing and speaking are different skills.

In speech, for example, extensive repetition and rephrasing are valuable tools to guide your listener to the gist of your message. Since the words you spoke just seconds before have disappeared into thin air, your listener must be continually reminded of the point you are making. Your business letter, on the other hand, is a visible record of your message. Your words are there in print—they won't evaporate. Thus if you have used the tools of speech when writing, your letter will be rambling, windy, and disjointed. It may *sound* clear to you, but it will *read* unclear to the recipient. At best, the reader will be distracted by the excess words and, at worst, angered at your seeming inability to get to the point. The widespread use of dictating machines makes it doubly important that you remember you are writing a letter and not delivering a speech. How, then, do you give the appearance of a "natural-sounding" letter without actually transcribing speech?

Be concise. Short sentences and brief paragraphs free the reader from rambling thoughts that point him in many directions but ultimately lead him nowhere. We ramble in print because we don't know what we want to say, we don't know how to say it, or we want to say too much all at once. By forcing yourself to use compact sentences, you are in fact forcing yourself to sort out and organize your thoughts. Don't do your thinking in the letter to the reader. Think first, then write.

Be direct. Deliver the point of the letter quickly by avoiding a long windup. The reader has no doubt waited several days for your reply. Now is not the time to tell him, "We are in receipt of your letter of June 23." He knows you got his letter because he is reading your reply. If the letter continues, "You requested a catalog of our latest Foam Floor line of resilient sheet flooring," he is going to become impatient. Start right off by answering his request, "The Foam Floor catalog you requested on June 23 should reach you within a few days." Retain directness throughout the body of the letter by stating your actions or requests simply. If they are well reasoned, they will produce the response you want. If not, all the qualifying and rephrasing in the world won't help them.

Be courteous. Few who write business letters intend to be discourteous to their readers. Most know that the insulting letter from an angry customer requires an especially tactful and courteous reply. Most impoliteness in print is inadvertent; nonetheless, it does you or your company no good. It generally happens because the writer forgets about the reader. He is thinking about a thing—the letter he must write—instead of the person who will read it. If you try to keep your reader in mind, you will answer him promptly and completely. He will then know that you read his letter carefully and gave it your immediate attention. He will be pleased because he will believe you are responding to him as a person. People like that. They can even be satisfied by a form letter if the letter answers their questions or solves their problem. The form letter has rankled legions of readers as "impersonal" not because it is mass printed or not specifically addressed but because the person who stuffed it in the envelope didn't read the customer's letter. The customer has waited over a week and received an answer to a question he didn't ask.

As you can see, conciseness, directness, and courtesy are not hard and fast rules but guidelines that will help you to write letters with clarity and proper tone. You now know generally what tack you will take to make your statement; you must next determine what you are going to say. How are these guidelines applied to specific letter-writing situations?

To respond to any letter you must first determine what kind of letter you will write. Will you be refusing credit, requesting an interview, turning down a job applicant? All three of these letters will be direct, concise, and courteous, but your emphasis must be specific to each problem. For example, if refusing credit, you may find it helpful to play heavily on courtesy, perhaps even occasionally sacrificing some directness. You would not say, for instance, "We can't grant you credit because your credit rating is poor," direct though that may be. What would you say? Let's look at the type of letters you will be called upon to write, how they differ, and how to handle them.

Start by asking yourself a few questions:

1. In this letter am I able to do what the reader wants me to do? Will this message please him?
2. Must I tell him no, disappoint him in some way?
3. Must I persuade him to do something he may not want to do? Must I sell him an idea, a product, or a service?

Questions like these will help you see that letters fall into three general categories: the "yes" letter, the "no" letter, and the "please do something" letter.

A "yes" letter tells the reader you will do as he asks, adjust his complaint in a favorable manner, or supply him with information which will benefit him in some way. The reader will be pleased. All routine good-news and goodwill letters are "yes" letters.

A "no" letter does the opposite. In it you must tell the reader that you cannot do as he would like. The reader will not be pleased. As you might imagine, bad-news letters are the most difficult to write. The best reaction you can hope for is the reader's acceptance and continued goodwill, however grudging. Some letters in this category are credit refusals, job rejections, and refusals of requests for time and money.

The "please do something" letter, broadly defined, includes all those letters of persuasion you are called upon to write. In this letter you try to talk somebody into doing something—usually something that will benefit you, and often something that will benefit you more than it may the reader. Included here are sales letters (please buy this product or service); the job application (please interview me); the persuasive request (please help with your time, money, your good name); and the collection letter (please pay your bill).

SECTION 2

How to Write a "Yes" Letter

The easiest letter to write is the one in which you tell somebody you will do what he wants you to do: you will send his catalogs, or answer his question, or enclose his check.

To get started make a list of the things you must include. A subject line (see section 6) may help you begin a "yes" letter. After you've decided what points you intend to cover in the letter, go directly to the good news. "The gun you are interested in, Mr. Booth, is described on page 9 of the enclosed catalog." Try to avoid warming up with remarks like "This will acknowledge your request of August 15." Sentences like these put the reader off; they sound distant and stuffy and don't really tell him anything.

In the body of the letter, supply as much detail as the reader will need to solve his problem. Since you've decided to answer his question, you don't want to sound curt by giving him an evasive, incomplete, or sketchy answer. On the other hand, don't be afraid to write a short letter—perhaps only several sentences—if it does the job. Curtness is not the result of brevity but of incompleteness.

When it comes time to end the letter, do so. Don't be the guest who came for dinner and stayed all week. Say "Goodnight" and leave. End graciously: "If you have other questions, please write again." Try to avoid rubber-stamp constructions: "Hoping this explanation will solve your problem, I am. . . ," "Please feel free. . . ," "Don't hesitate to. . . ." On the other hand, don't try too hard to be fresh and original. A few time-honored clichés do no great harm in a good-news letter and will probably sound more natural and unobtrusive than a strained attempt at something creative.

Throughout the letter, keep the tone immediate by focusing on the reader rather than on you or your company. For example, compare the following two sentences:

> You are certainly correct, Mr. Tweeter, that a worn or damaged stylus can ruin your records.
>
> We at Jewel Tip Stylus and Cartridge, Inc., have conclusively determined that a worn or damaged stylus can ruin records.

No reader could help reacting more favorably to the first example. After all, he is the subject of the entire sentence. In addition, his view of reality is reinforced when he is told, "You are correct." Using *your* in front of *records* further personalizes the statement; you are worried about *his* records. Of course, you are also capitalizing on his original concern for the condition of his discs that motivated his letter to you. The second example does not present the information in a form with which the reader can easily identify. An amorphous blob of corporate facelessness ("We at Jewel Tip Stylus and Cartridge, Inc.") is just not a warm and human image. Start now consciously to rework your sentences so that they emphasize the reader and his concerns. Most people place themselves at the forefront of their writing, saying "*I* think you are right" instead of "*You* are right." To keep the reader in the spotlight, use *you* and *your* and avoid *we* and *I* as much as possible. It is a valuable habit to develop, for no device is more successful in setting and maintaining the proper tone in business letters than the skillful use of this *you* attitude.

In a competitive world you learn to look out for yourself or you don't survive—or at least you don't prosper. So our self-interest is a constant preoccupation. We write a letter because we have a problem. We want somebody (the reader) to do something, to understand our point of view, to cooperate, to make the world a little safer for us. Examine any letter and you will see readily the interest of the writer.

The reader, however, is in this world too. He is concerned about his own survival, his own prosperity, more than he is about yours. Accordingly, when you write a letter, think of the interest of the reader and address that interest. Make the letter respond to the question "What's in this for my reader?"

Perhaps the most troublesome "yes" letter to write is one that requires a fairly complex answer. Your best bet in this case is to get to know the reader from his letter. People often tell you a lot about themselves in their letters: "As a college student. . . ," "Like most housewives, I. . . ," "I read in *House Splendid* the other day. . . ." There are other clues. Look at the address. Warm or cold climate? In the East, the South, Texas? Metropolitan, suburban, or rural area? If you're familiar with the town, of course, you know even more about him. Is the letter typed or handwritten? Is it neat or sloppy? Examine the signature— Mr., Miss, Mrs., or Ms.? Is he or she a professional (M.D., J.D., D.O., R.N.) or in a branch of the armed services (Pvt. George I. Joseph)? Does he use any terminology that might indicate the extent of his familiarity with your product or service? Does he seem to know anything at all about the production process? Finding out as much as you can about him will not only give you an idea of how detailed your answer should be but will also aid you in responding to him in a more personal way.

Many businesses and institutions have fliers or brochures explaining a system, process, or method they are often asked about: "Points to Remember When Selecting an Oscilloscope," "Rooming-In: At Home in the Maternity Ward," "Mulching Your Garden with Black Plastic." Frequently, these pamphlets contain illustrations, pictures, diagrams, and graphs that aid the reader and that would be impossible for you to duplicate in a letter. So by all means make use of such materials if they are available. Just make sure that the answer to the customer's question is in the flier you send him. You may be able to convince yourself that the answer *surely* must be in one of the three pamphlets you stuffed in the envelope; but if it isn't, the reader won't be fooled. He'll be angry. It is simply bad business to send the hothouse orchid grower who needs technical advice on humidity control your pamphlet "Redwood Window Boxes—Getting Started with Flowers" and to figure you have taken care of his request.

Whenever you send a pamphlet or flier, you can make your response more personal for the recipient with a brief cover letter. A cover letter directs the reader to the material you have enclosed and, when it is not obvious, explains why you have included it. Use the cover letter to introduce the reader to the material you have sent him.

> You will find a list showing dealer cost and suggested retail price for all currently manufactured Glowmore receiving tubes in this handy "Glowmore Tube Price Manual."

If you send a lengthy pamphlet, direct the reader to the section or pages he will need.

> The lubrication points for Swirl-Air circulating fan, Model 703, are shown on page 6 of the enclosed pamphlet, "Maintenance Procedures for Swirl-Air 700 Series Fans."

Feel free to use form letters if you must respond to many similar requests. Your correspondent understands that routine requests are often handled efficiently with form letters. A well-crafted form letter will not seem inappropriate to him if it applies to his situation. Be sure that it does.

Points to Remember

Granting the Request

1. Read correspondent's letter carefully. Make sure you understand what he wants.
2. Get to the point quickly. Don't be afraid to jump right into the meat of the letter.
3. Avoid worn-out expressions like "In reply to yours of the 14th instant . . ." or even "I have received your letter of the 14th."
4. Make the letter direct, brief, easy to read.
5. Aim explanations at the level of the reader as you perceive it from his letter to you. Never talk down to or "snow" the reader.
6. Adopt *you* attitude to avoid a stuffy, "front office" tone.
7. Consider using lists for steps or directions.

8. Sell your product or service if it is appropriate. Make your sales message specific to his situation.
9. Don't be afraid to stop when you've said all you have to say. Offer further help only if you are willing to give it.

Writing the Goodwill Letter

1. Make sure proper tone permeates this letter.
2. Be friendly, personal, *you*-oriented.
3. Avoid a breezy style.
4. Be brief, direct.
5. If making an announcement, include all necessary details.

SECTION 3

How to Write a "No" Letter

A "no" letter is difficult to write because in it you must make two apparently contradictory points. First, you have to tell the reader you will not do what he wants you to do. Second, you hope to retain his goodwill.

Begin by assuming that in most cases the request is a reasonable one from an honorable person. If at first his claim sounds unjustified to you, remember that he probably wouldn't have written if he didn't think he had a good case. Even if the claim appears blatantly dishonest or the request ridiculous, you lose nothing, since you are saying no anyway, by being tactful and courteous. Often requests that seem absurd to us are seen as completely justified by the people making them. We may know something they don't; they may have misunderstood our position. In any case, our job is to show our side, clearly and reasonably, and to appeal to their sense of fair play.

Fix in your mind the effect you would like your letter to have. Show the reader you are a reasonable person. If you set the tone of reason and goodwill, he is more apt to respond in a like manner. Let the reader know that you would do what he wants if you could but that you can't do it for a good reason. Then show him that reason. If you do your job well, he can agree that in your shoes he would do like-wise. And you can't beat that.

The letter may open in one of two ways: the *direct refusal* or the *delayed refusal*. If you are the kind of person who prefers to shoot from the hip, you may feel more comfortable with the direct approach. With this method you deliver the bad news in the first sentence and then spend the rest of the letter trying to soften the blow. Here is an example of the direct refusal:

> Dear Mrs. Coffee:
>
> I certainly wish we could replace free of charge the Party-Size Perk Pot you returned to us for repair. We are always sorry when a customer has had bad luck with one of these fine appliances. That's why we had our laboratory examine it carefully for flaws in workmanship or materials. Unfortunately, the examination showed that the Perk Pot had been immersed in water, and no Perk Pot can stand that. That's why the instruction booklet and the little metal tag affixed to the bottom say, "Do not immerse in water." Frequently, an accident like this happens without the owner knowing how or even who is to blame.
>
> However, all is not lost. We are willing to share some of your misfortune. We can replace the heating element and seal for $8.75, which is our cost, and have the Party-Size Perk Pot back to you within the week. Please use the enclosed postal card to authorize a repair on this basis.

Although a direct refusal in the opening sentence may work, you may prefer to ease into the bad news after first getting on common ground and then presenting the reason for the refusal. Compare the following use of the delayed refusal with the direct example you just read:

> You are certainly right to expect more than three months service from your Party-Size Perk Pot. These fine appliances, properly used, have an average life of five to seven years before needing repair. That's why we can afford to have the most liberal guarantee in the small appliance industry against breakdown from normal wear.
>
> An examination of your Perk Pot, however, shows that it has been damaged by the one misfortune no percolator manufacturer can guarantee against—the damage that comes from immersion in water. That's why. . . .

From here on the letter can be pretty much like the first one.

In most cases the delayed refusal has advantages. Job and credit refusals are most harsh-sounding without a buffer of some sort to cushion the bad news. Often you can find something good to say or some way to compliment the reader in the first sentence. Just be careful not to mislead the reader into thinking you will grant the request.

In the job refusal, for example, say something pleasant about your interview with the prospect: "I certainly enjoyed the talk we had last Thursday in which we discussed your desire to become a surveyor." Then lead into the bad news. If you can encourage him to apply at a future date, let the construction of your sentence emphasize the hopeful aspects of your message and subordinate the refusal. For instance, the sentence "While I cannot offer you the position we discussed, I hope you will contact me in the early spring when we expect to have two openings in related employment" says the same thing as the following statement, but says it less harshly. You could have said, "I am unable to offer you the position we discussed on Thursday. If you are available in the early spring, I hope you will contact me again. I expect to have two similar openings then." The messages are identical. However, since you can offer him hope for future employment, let this good news shoulder the bad, as in the first example. There is no need to make an honest expectation of future employment sound like a rejection.

Suppose, however, that not only must you refuse him the job but that you also can give him no encouragement about a future position with your company or firm. You can still use sentence structure to mute the turndown; you can still wish him good luck. "While I cannot offer you a position as an accountant with Debit Brothers, I hope you soon find employment and go on to a rewarding career."

When refusing credit, too, remember that although you must write a "no" letter, the letter itself need not be completely negative. Perhaps you are unable to extend credit, but you can offer to continue doing business on a cash basis. The delayed refusal allows you to begin with a positive tone:

Dear Mr. Volt:

Your decision to enter the growing television and radio repair business is good news to us at Zap Electronics Distributors. In addition to sharing common interests in a rapidly advancing field, our competent salespeople look forward to supplying you with the test equipment and parts you will need to get your business going.

As you know, the financial burdens of beginning any business, particularly one as complex and changing as electronics, are substantial. We have had the experience of extending credit to new customers to help them get their business going only to find we had done them a disservice. For in the early months the young businesses did not generate enough servicing volume to meet the demand that large credit purchases placed on them.

Let's help each other by dealing on a cash basis, at least for a few months. As a dealer, you are welcome to attend our annual show, April 14, 7 to 9 p.m., at the Watts Avenue store. In the meantime, you can count on our large in-store inventory and direct factory ordering to get the parts you need in your hands as quickly as possible.

Notice the attempt in this letter to turn the refusal of credit into a service to the customer. Such reasoning is not so farfetched as it may appear. If you have a good reason for not granting credit to someone, and you do it anyway, you run the risk not only of losing your money but also of placing the customer in a financial bind he cannot get out of. This is a disservice to him. Let him see that it is to his advantage not to use credit buying with your company at this time. To tell your reader that "company policy" does not permit you to grant his request is to give him no answer at all. It is an evasion and he knows it. He has no chance to see your company or firm as one making careful decisions based on experience and logical thinking. A company that can't supply good reasons in refusing reasonable requests from its customers will soon have no customers.

As you can see, the prerequisites to writing a successful "no" letter include sounding as positive as possible under the circumstances, being sympathetic and understanding, and showing that you have an honest and sincere interest in the reader's problem.

Points to Remember

Refusing a Claim or Adjustment

1. Read correspondent's letter carefully to discover what you can about him and his understanding of your product or service.
2. Adapt your letter in tone and content to his level of understanding. Avoid the extremes of talking down to the reader or "snowing" him with technical language.

3. Delay your refusal. Open with an empathetic, soothing tone.
4. Try to agree with the customer about *something* in the opening. At least begin on common, neutral ground. Don't, however, mislead him into thinking you'll make the adjustment.
5. Adopt *you* attitude in the opening.
6. Give a sensible, reasonable explanation for the refusal. Don't blame it on "company policy."
7. Whenever possible avoid leading into the refusal with negative terms like *unfortunately*.
8. State the refusal as positively as possible. Tell what you can do rather than what you cannot do. Often you can avoid saying what you won't do.

> So you can get the freshest candies at the lowest price, Chewy Nuggets are sold through local retailers only.

9. Don't dwell on the bad news. Be clear, direct, and brief.
10. Don't apologize. If your reason is good, you shouldn't have to.
11. Give helpful suggestions when you can: Is there any way the customer can remedy the situation himself? Can you think of alternative courses he might explore?
12. Never accuse. Avoid expressions like *you state* and *your mistake*.
13. Always give the reader an out. Don't rob him of his pride.
14. Never be sarcastic. Don't try to score points.
15. Be well-reasoned and courteous.
16. Don't rub the reader's nose in his own mistakes or shortcomings. If he mishandled a product or situation, say briefly what he should have done.
17. Use care in ending your letter that you don't invite the problem back or provoke the reader's scorn. A refusal, for example, is usually not the place to end with "If I can be of any future help. . . ."
18. Be wary of using resale of product or service in a refusal letter. Most often it is inappropriate here.
19. End on a neutral or upbeat note. Pick up the common ground you established in the opening or change the subject.

Refusing a Request

1. Establish courteous tone, *you* attitude. You can, perhaps, thank the correspondent for thinking of you, your product or service.

2. Give a good reason for the refusal. A single good reason is better than ten bad ones.
3. State the refusal as positively as possible. If you can offer suggestions, subordinate the turndown to any help you can give.

   While we cannot supply your club with a speaker, you might find that our slide presentation "Reclaiming Strip-Mined Land" would make an equally informative program.

4. Don't overapologize. A good reason is the best apology.
5. Offer any assistance you are prepared to give.
6. End on a positive note. Often you can express good wishes for the success of the event or venture.

SECTION 4

How to Write a "Please Do Something" Letter

You want somebody to do something for you or your company—speak to your group, have a look at your invention, endorse your proposal, finance your project, stock your new line. How do you write to persuade someone to do what you want?

Think about the person who can best fill your needs. Often you know who this will be. If so, you will be gearing your letter to your motorcycle dealer in the Southwest, or to your product representative in New York, or to the Kiwanis Club president. In petitioning for someone's time or skill, your problem is more difficult when you're not sure whom you should ask. Perhaps you're afraid you'll seem presumptuous if you ask the person you really want. Maybe you've ruled him out because you figured he'd be too busy. Don't assume that a person is unreachable just because he is famous. The campus beauty queen sometimes spends a lonely Saturday night because half of the boys are sure she must already have been asked and the other half are certain she would refuse them if they did ask. Winston Churchill made his famous "Iron Curtain" speech at an American college. Harvard? Yale? Princeton? No. It was Westminster College, Fulton, Missouri. Why did the man of the century accept an invitation to speak at a little college in Middle America? There must have been something in it for him.

That's a good place to start. Why should this person do what you ask him to do? Try to put yourself in the reader's place—whether it's the chairman of the Interstate Commerce Commission or a housewife. Ask yourself the questions he or she might ask: What will I get? What will I have to do to get it? Weighed against all other opportunities, why is this one best?

In most cases calling for persuasion, you can make accurate guesses about the probable answers to questions like these if you know enough about your subject. In direct mail campaigns you can preselect your readers according to sex, income, geographical area, political affiliation, magazines they subscribe to, new cars they may have purchased, organizations they belong to, charities they contribute to, and so on. Very likely your readers fall into several categories. Make use of what you know. Make sensible guesses about their situation from the information you have. If you are selling diaper service to new mothers, you can assume they'd rather not wash diapers if they had a choice, that diaper-pail odors are a problem they must deal with, that they love their babies and want to put germ-free diapers on them, and that they are worried about rashes their baby might get from diapers washed in harsh detergents.

If you are dealing with a prominent person, make it your business to find out all you can about him. Study his life style, read his speeches, read his books. A famous poet was persuaded to make a round trip from Spain to read his poems at a large state university not because he looked forward to literary discussions with the faculty and students but because he had heard about the university's work with mushrooms, a subject that interested him greatly. Like the poet, most of us agree to do things—speak at your luncheon, buy your product—when it is in our own self-interest to do so. If you can discover that interest and appeal to it, you are well on your way.

Here are some points to keep in mind as you write your "please do something" letter:

1. Don't use a subject line. It is inappropriate here and would put the reader off.
2. Begin and end on a note of reader interest—what you perceive as the most promising motivating interest.
3. Justify your request. Tell what is at stake.
4. Picture the reader doing the thing with pleasure.

5. Tell him how much you can pay him and/or the other advantages that will result.
6. Don't promise too much—certainly not so much that the reader, if he accepts, will later be disappointed or disillusioned.
7. Reassure the reader about possible negative aspects or his special requirements in confidential or security matters.
8. Be careful with compliments. People don't object to them, but they may object to flattery.

In a "please do something" letter, as in a "yes" letter, you will want to make a conscious effort to use the reader's point of view throughout. You will want to say, in effect, "You are the person we want to head our charity drive" instead of "We would like you. . . ." You will put the emphasis on the reader's needs if you say, "Your dog will be the healthy, handsome pet you want him to be with just two drops of Mange-Away added to his food daily." He will see that you are more concerned with featuring the name of your product if you phrase thoughts like the one above by writing, "Mange-Away will help your dog become the healthy. . . ."

A word of caution here. Making a letter, particularly the direct mail sales letter, sound "personal" to the reader does not mean the gimmicky inclusion of his name between commas three times throughout the text of the sales pitch. Nor does typing the name of his hometown into the space provided for it in line seven lull him into the delusion that your message is aimed at him alone. People are not idiots. In fact, they are very nearly experts on unsolicited mail—they get so much of it so often. The reader will be looking at your service or product to see how it will solve his problems. He will think your letter is "personal" if it accurately identifies his situation and shows him how he can benefit from your service or product.

Points to Remember

Writing a Persuasive Request

1. Rely heavily on *you* attitude. It is crucial in this letter that you show the reader what's in it for him.
2. While you may want to use the delayed opening to strengthen your position, don't take too long getting to the point.

3. Give supporting reasons justifying the request. Avoid, however, dwelling on explanations that tell the reader how his cooperation will solve *your* problem.
4. Make certain you include all the details explaining what you want him to do or how he should proceed.
5. Since you are asking the reader to *do* something, make it convenient for him to comply.
6. Be reassuring and cooperative. Avoid expressions of doubt like *if all goes well*.
7. In your eagerness to persuade, be careful not to make wild promises or unsubstantiated claims.
8. Never beg or grovel.
9. End by giving the reader a picture of himself doing as you ask and benefiting from it. Use words that assume he'll comply (without, of course, sounding presumptuous).

> NOT: If you will simply check the item marked. . . .
> BUT: Simply check the item marked. . . .

Writing a Sales Letter

1. Be sure your opening attracts favorable attention by making some appropriate remark aimed at the reader's needs or wants. Study the opening lines of sales letters and notice the way writers try to get the reader's attention.
2. Create a desire for the item or concept you are selling. Show the reader profitably or pleasurably using your item or service.
3. Try to convince the reader that this one product is the one to buy at this time. It is not enough to create desire for a typewriter if the reader then hunts through the want ads to buy a secondhand one at a cheap price. Make him want yours, now. Marshal all the appeals you can. Know whether you are making rational or emotional appeals.
4. Minimize difficulties. Show why it is better to make the move now for this product.
5. Ask for appropriate action. Do you want the reader to return a postcard, make a phone call, go to his nearest dealer? Whatever it is, ask for it with confidence and good taste.
6. In all these matters, operate within your honest view of the reader's best interest. If you have enthusiasm for your product or service, how can you help your potential customer share the pleasure you know he will have owning the thing you sell?

Writing a Collection Letter

1. Decide what stage your collection effort is in, whether you think the debtor intends to pay or not.
2. If it is an early effort (30, 60, even 90 days are usually in the notification or the reminder stage), send out the statement with the words *reminder* or *past due* or *please* added to it.
3. At some point, depending on the nature of your business and the type of clientele, you must decide whether or not you as creditor have a right to worry. You are now not so sure the debtor intends to pay. You can ask him. Remind him of the transaction, the agreement, the long silence. You can say, "I wish you would tell me: Do you intend to pay?" "Possibly you have had bad luck," and so on.
4. If the inquiry does not get results, you can begin a series of appeals—to fair play, to keeping a good credit rating, to being an honest person. Some experts believe the only real appeal is an appeal to fear—and that the fear of losing one's job is the greatest. If you can make the appeal without breaking any laws you can get results. But the legal aspects of collection are a field of their own. Get legal advice before you make urgent appeals that might be regarded as threats.
5. The last step is to apply pressure with an ultimatum. For this you must first talk to your lawyer.

SECTION 5

How to Write a Job Application

People no longer write long, chronological letters of application. Instead, applications are broken in two—(1) the résumé, a personal data sheet, and (2) the covering letter. The résumé is a concise biography, a reference, and it remains essentially the same whether you are responding to an invitation to apply for a job or launching a direct mail campaign to scout out job possibilities. The covering letter highlights those items in your résumé that you believe will catch the interest of the prospective employer.

Source: Adapted from Earl P. Strong and Robert G. Weaver, *Writing for Business and Industry*, pp. 158–171. Copyright © 1962 by Allyn and Bacon, Inc. Used with permission.

The Résumé

Employers are interested primarily in three areas. (1) What kind of person are you? Family background, physical details, marital status, hobbies—the sort of thing that comes under the heading "Personal Information." Include in this section any details that present you as a normal, likable person. (2) What can you do? The answer to this question lies partly in your work experience, partly in the kind of person you are, and partly in your education and training. If you are beginning a career, your education will offer the most helpful clue to what you can do, and a prospective employer will carefully examine details in that category. If you already have significant work experience, a prospective employer will be more interested in the third area. (3) What will you be like on the job? This may be the most crucial area. You may have the potential—that is, the education and training sufficient to sell automobiles or manage a baseball team or whatever the position is—and still not be willing to do the job. For this reason the employer will be very much interested in your work experience. A very good way to discover what a person *will* do is to look carefully at what he has done.

In typing your résumé, make it easy to read. Pay attention to good visual presentation—arrangement of copy on the page, use of space, word economy. Try to present your history on one page. There is no arbitrary best arrangement. Take whatever liberties you need to present your qualifications in the most attractive format. Examples are shown in exhibits A and B.

The Covering Letter

As a job seeker, you now know how to construct a résumé. Next, you need to know how to write a good application letter to accompany it.

Many people send a letter saying in effect "I read your ad in the *Daily Astonisher;* please consider me an applicant for the job. Details of my experience and background are on the attached data sheet." Such a letter has one important virtue: it is short. But it is not so helpful as it might be. The letter can be short and still say something pertinent.

Your application letter has the same relationship to your résumé that a good, influential friend would have to you personally. In getting a job it would be ideal if your friend could lead you into the prospec-

Personal History
of
Eva A. Hutta
241 E. Prospect Avenue
State College, PA 16801
238-8256

July 28, 19--

EDUCATION 19-- to 19--	Liberty High School, Bethlehem, Pennsylvania; graduated June 19--.
19-- to present	The Pennsylvania State University; Business Education major. I expect to receive my Bachelor of Science degree in Education in June 19--.
EXPERIENCE Nov. 19-- to June 19--	I was employed by Orr's Department Store, Bethlehem, Pennsylvania, as an office clerk. My job included taking dictation, typing, filing, and working in the cash office.
June 19-- to Jan. 19--	I worked in the Central Transcribing Bureau of Bethlehem Steel Company, Bethlehem, Pennsylvania. I transcribed letters from dictaphone machines and spent some time working in the Labor-Management Relations Department as a stenographer-typist.
Summer of 19--	I was in charge of the office of Pottstown Community Camp, Earlville, Pennsylvania. I took dictation, typed, filed, kept the books, and handled the registration of campers.
Summer of 19--	Presently, while attending summer sessions at Penn State, I am employed part-time as a stenographer in Computation Services. My job consists of taking dictation, typing, and answering the telephone.
PERSONAL DETAILS	I am 20 years old, 5 feet 2 inches tall, weigh 123 pounds, have brown hair and eyes, and am in excellent health. At Penn State, I am a member of Theta Phi Alpha social sorority and enjoy swimming, bowling, tennis, and reading.
REFERENCES	Mr. Harold H. Thomas Mr. Joseph Gribbin Central Transcribing Bureau Liberty High School Bethlehem Steel Company Bethlehem, PA 18015 701 East Third Street Bethlehem, PA 18015 Mr. William Welsh Pottstown Community Camp Earlville, PA 19519

EXHIBIT A. SAMPLE RESUME TO ACCOMPANY AN APPLICATION LETTER

John Axel Thrustor

118 E. College Avenue
Center City, PA 16801

24 years old
5' 10"
135 pounds

Married (no children)

Academic Training

3 1/2 years (19-- - 19--) at Central State University, majoring in English
Composition. "A" average in English courses taken, including Biography,
The Short Story, Technique, Criticism, and Exposition.

1 year at the University of Utah, majoring in Commercial Art.
(19-- - 19--)

2 years at the Maryland Institute of Art, majoring in Illustration.
(19-- - 19--)

Military Training

2 years in Army Signal Corps.
14 months as chief of an Air-Ground Liaison Team.
Communications Expert (rating).

Practical Training (Work Experience) 19-- - 19--.

Editor, Central State Fun (campus humor magazine) 19--.

Head Waiter and Social Director at the Willow Dell House (Pocono
Mountain resort) 19--.

Encyclopedia Salesman for P. F. Collier, Inc. 19--.

Painter, Machinist's Assistant at How-Ell-Dor Manufacturing Co., Paoli,
Pennsylvania 19--.

University Activities and Organizations

2-year starter on Lacrosse Team
Varsity Letter Club
Belles Lettres
Lacrosse Club (vice-president)
Art & Editorial staffs of Central State Fun
Druids (men's honorary society)

EXHIBIT B. SAMPLE RESUME SHOWING ANOTHER FORMAT

tive employer's office and say "Here, Mr. Winters, is a good man, a good worker, strongly qualified for the job that's open. Talk with him and give him every possible consideration." If your friend were able to support such an opening with specific details, you must agree that you would be off to a good start in your interview. Consider some of the effects that your friend might accomplish: he would attract favorable attention to you, supply evidence of your outstanding qualifications, sharpen certain strong points in your background. He could overcome certain deficiencies you may have, speak the language of the employer—work-centered language—and ask for appropriate action.

Most of the time you won't have influential friends in the right places, and your initial contact won't be made in person; so you send in your place the paper image of you in capsule form—the résumé. The letter that accompanies the paper image must do for it what your good friend would do for you.

Attract Attention

Remember that a job is open because the employer believes that the person who fills it will make more money for the company—or save more money—than the company will have to pay to that person in salary. So, to attract favorable attention, your opening paragraph must say something to convey the idea that you can do a good job. This is especially true when you are prospecting with an unsolicited letter.

Following are a few openings that might be expected to attract favorable attention. They are not to be copied word for word. In writing your own, strive for freshness and originality. However, you may be able to adapt these examples in original ways to suit your own purposes after you understand the appeals involved.

> With my college major in accounting and three summers' experience in the accounting department of the Newton Machine Company, I believe I am qualified to fill the position in your cost accounting department.
>
> For several years I have had as my goal a position selling farm machinery for a top-ranking company. After you have examined my qualifications, I think that you will agree that I am ready.

A direct, confident opening such as the latter is good, if you have the evidence to support the claim that you are ready. Employers often like a statement of a goal. It shows that you understand yourself and know where you want to go. Here is another work-centered opening that would probably attract attention.

> For the past three years, while I was studying sales management in night school, I worked as a clerk in the Goodstone Tire and Rubber Company store here in Centerville. Now that I have my degree and a lot of valuable experience, I feel ready to put it all to good use as a store manager anywhere there may be an opening in your organization. Please consider my qualifications.

If you have been fortunate enough to learn about the job from a person known and respected by the prospective employer, by all means use the name to attract favorable attention.

> Mr. Harold Hicks of your credit department told me this morning that you need a job analyst—one who has a thorough knowledge of the techniques of job analysis, an appreciation of the importance of good human relations in carrying them out, and a desire for a permanent career in the personnel field. If you will examine the attached résumé and consider the following statements, I think you will agree that I have the qualifications.

Provide Evidence

If you have written a successful opening, you have interested your reader. He wants to see some evidence. A few sentences pointing out a particularly strong item of experience or training are in order. Make the most of your unique background; be brief but positive. You can do a good job here if you will take a few minutes to study the position under consideration. Study the ad—or better yet, study the job specification if it is available. Then, in parallel columns, make a list: What do they seem to want? What can I offer?

This kind of analysis can be fun. Examine closely three or four ads for apparently identical jobs and you will find that the various employers seem to stress different qualifications. It would be a mistake to send them identical letters on the assumption that the positions are the same.

One ad will be vaguely worded, inviting applications from "bright," "aggressive," people with "initiative and ability to meet career opportunity head on." Another ad will stress the need for a "recent, mature college graduate" with a "degree in business administration or psychology." Another will put heavier emphasis on related experience, work you have done, and so on.

By studying the various advertisements or job specifications, you can often find subtle indications of "what they seem to want." Then by studying your résumé—which, you remember, is you in capsule form—you can often find some experience or course that can be pointed out to your advantage.

Remember that *all* work experience is valuable. Don't apologize or fail to mention it just because the job didn't last long or you weren't paid much. Don't say, "The only experience I ever had directing the work of others was ten years ago when I was in the army and led a platoon of disabled soldiers through limited calisthenics." Say instead, "While I was in the army I learned a great deal about the principles of leadership in the challenging task of leading disabled soldiers through calisthentics."

If there is one qualification that seems to be most important to a particular job, emphasize that qualification first and most strongly. If possible, show some knowledge of the company.

Ask for Appropriate Action

The purpose of the application letter is not to get a job, but to get an interview. Nobody will hire you sight unseen. Therefore, the appropriate action that you want from your letter is a job interview. Ask for it:

> I shall be in Pittsburgh from September first through the tenth. May I see you at your convenience during that period?
>
> Please suggest a time when you can conveniently allow me to discuss my qualifications further.
>
> I should appreciate an opportunity to come to your office for an interview at your convenience.

The Complete Letter

The application letter should be slanted to each particular job. To succeed, it should be brief; it should attract favorable attention; it should sharpen your outstanding qualifications; it should turn liabilities into assets; it should ask for appropriate action.

Here is one example of a complete letter. The young woman who wrote it directed it to a specific job. Had she been writing for a different job, she would have changed the emphasis accordingly.

> Mr. Thomas H. Elliott, who is in charge of the Central Transcribing Bureau in your organization, told me this morning that he believes I should qualify for the position of secretary to the sales manager.
>
> Because I worked for the Hometown Steel Company during summer vacations in 19— and 19—, I am already familiar with the typing and filing formats used, and I am well acquainted with company policy in other respects. My appointment would, therefore, save the company valuable training time and expense.
>
> As a business education major, I have a wide knowledge of business subjects. I can take dictation at the rate of 120 words a minute, file neatly, compose effective business letters, operate several business machines, and handle routine office situations adequately and confidently.
>
> The attached personal history will give you details about my work experience, education, and personal qualifications.
>
> May I come in to see you at your convenience and answer any questions you might have?

The Application Blank

If an employer becomes interested in you at all, he will almost certainly ask you to fill out a company application blank. Even though he has all the information in your résumé and letter of application, it is standard procedure for him to want to see how you look on his own form. Filling out the average application blank is a deadly bore, especially after you spent so much time on your résumé. The irritation doubles each time you must do the unpleasant chore.

Because of this irritation, many people fill out the blank hastily, and this is a serious mistake. Among more careful personnel people, the application is not just a piece of paper with some writing on it— something to fill a manila folder. It is a document as carefully devised as an FBI security check. Hasty, careless answers can ruin your chances. That is why some applicants request an additional copy so that they can have a typist neatly insert their carefully constructed answers. Let's take a look at the booby traps contained in a typical application blank for a sales position.

QUESTION	SIGNIFICANCE
What is your present address?	Is it a desirable neighborhood? Is it consistent with income?
Why are you applying for this position?	Do you have a definite goal? Are the reasons practical?
How did you secure the last position?	Were you trying to get into sales? Did you show ingenuity or self-reliance?
Why did you leave the last job?	Are the reasons acceptable? Do they check with the records?
What did you like about your position?	Have you been happy in your past selling work?
What did you dislike?	Did you get along with people? Were you loyal to your employer?

Careless answers here could be disastrous.

Follow-up Letters

It would be a good idea to keep a record of your job applications. A notebook with headings such as "Name of Company," "Date of Application," "Type of Application" (prospecting or invited), and "Follow-up" would be an excellent tool. Then, if there are any companies you especially want to work for, you should write follow-up letters.

Soon after an interview, while the experience is still fresh, you may want to compose a letter identifying the advantages the prospective employer would have if he offered you the job. The writer of the following letter feels his particular strengths are his wide experience in purchasing and the cooperation of his present boss.

> Thank you for the time you gave me during our interview yesterday. I am very grateful for the opportunity to present my qualifications to you in person.
>
> The outline of your company that you gave me has firmly convinced me that being associated with it would be most advantageous from the standpoint of both present and future possibilities. Because of the wide experience I have had in purchasing, I feel certain that a rapid adjustment could be made, and that within a short time I could be effectively producing for you.

My present employer knows of our interview. He has indicated that he would like to have me stay with him, but because of business conditions he is unable to offer me the salary he believes I merit. Therefore, he will release me from my present duties July 1, if I hear favorably from you.

If the first follow-up letter does not get you the job, one more try several months later may. Personnel people are human, too. They like to solve their problems with as little trouble as possible. Their success depends on getting the best people available. They do keep your application on file. They are sorry that they can't use you immediately; if they could, it would solve a problem for them, and they don't like to have problems. But they may forget how wonderful you are in a few months and, if a job suddenly develops for someone with your qualifications, there is no guarantee that they will immediately think of you. Instead, they may take the first good person who comes along. If you are eager to work for a certain company, write a letter several months after your original application.

In June I applied for a position as _____ with your company. Since that time, I have been working part time as a _____ and this experience has increased my enthusiasm for working for you. I hope that you will keep my application in your active file. [Or—Please review my application and let me know if you now need someone with my qualifications.]

Letter Accepting a Job

In writing a letter accepting a job, you need do little more than confirm the facts of the offer, the conditions under which you accept, and the date on which you will report. The little more that you must do is to make certain the employer will feel good about offering you the job. A bit of enthusiasm and confidence may be in order.

I was delighted this morning to receive your letter offering me a position in your cost accounting department. Of the several attractive job opportunities I've had, this is the one I most wanted. I am happy to accept it.

The conditions of my appointment as outlined in your letter are reasonable, and I should like to assure you that you will have my full cooperation as we work together.

I am pleased, too, that you are giving me until June 14 to report. After four years of twelve-hour study days, a brief vacation will be very welcome; so unless you tell me otherwise, I'll see you at eight o'clock on the fourteenth.

Letter Refusing a Job

In the happy event that you have been offered two jobs, take as much care refusing the one as you do accepting the other. Don't gloat over the better offer or belittle the poorer one. You want the employer you refuse to feel that he has just missed landing an excellent addition to his staff, that you are exactly the kind of person he wants, and that if you are ever available in the future he would want you. You never know.

My visit with you and the Operations Committee at New Hall was one of the most stimulating job contacts I've had.

The opportunity you offer me to travel among your several plants, setting up training programs for supervisors, certainly is an attractive one. However, as I mentioned during our talks, my main interests are in the general field of personnel management. For this reason, I have accepted a job that will give me experience in labor relations, personnel recruiting, and wage and salary administration, as well as employee training.

Your plan to select instructors from the ranks is a good one, I think, and I shall be watching its development with a great deal of interest.

Points to Remember

1. Know yourself well enough to know what jobs you can do and which ones you can apply for with any hope of success.
2. Apply in two parts—a résumé and a covering letter.
3. Use a good model for the format of your résumé. Make sure your application stands out in some way.
4. Consider using professional help to get an effective job-application package.
5. Avoid slang and be wary of attempts at humor.
6. Since your résumé is you in capsule form, be sure it includes all pertinent information on personal details, work experience, and

education. If possible include eventual job goals. Try to hold it to one page.

7. Don't leave any unexplained gaps in accounting for years in the résumé. The reader will wonder what you did during the unaccounted-for period.

8. In the covering letter, be as specific as you can be. Relate yourself in capsule form (the résumé) to the needs of the job opening.

9. To prepare the covering letter, make a list of what you think they want in the person they will hire. Then try to find qualities in your own life and work that would meet their wants. Write your letter to make full use of these qualities, treating them in the right order with the right emphasis.

10. Since your job-application letter is a sales letter, you must attract favorable attention, provide evidence, and ask for an interview. Its specific aim is to get an interview.

SECTION 6

How to Make Your Letters Attractive and Correct

A customer or client will form impressions about you and your company from the letter you send him. A colleague or superior will form opinions about your competence from the letter he gets from you. You are responsible for the letter you sign. You've got a lot to lose if your letter antagonizes a customer or offends a superior. Pay close attention to the details of letter appearance and correctness to be sure you are not overlooking a potential gaffe.

Making a Letter Attractive

Stationery Standards

The length of your letter will in large part determine the stationery you will use. Standard sizes of writing paper are measured in inches:

Letter size	$8\frac{1}{2} \times 11$
Legal size	$8\frac{1}{2} \times 13$
Half sheet	$8\frac{1}{2} \times 5\frac{1}{2}$
Note size	$5\frac{1}{2} \times 8\frac{1}{2}$
Official size (Monarch)	7×10
Government size	$8 \times 10\frac{1}{2}$

The traditional "letter size" is normally used for all but very short business letters. These are usually typed on half sheets or note-size paper. Envelopes are made in standard sizes too. Be sure to use the size that matches your writing paper.

You may use any color and weight paper that is appropriate to your needs. However, a high-quality white paper, a sixteen- to twenty-pound bond with a smooth finish, is always correct. Thinner, less expensive papers, often tinted or color coded for interoffice use, are generally used for carbon copies.

Margins and Spacing

Your letters should look as balanced and as pleasing as framed pictures. In a short letter the margins will be relatively wide; in a long letter, relatively narrow. Don't make them narrower than $1\frac{1}{4}$ inches from the right or left edge of the paper. Top and bottom margins are determined by the length of the message too. See exhibit C.

Don't type closer than $1\frac{1}{2}$ inches from the bottom of the page. If there is no letterhead, allow the same margin at the top. If there is a letterhead, begin far enough below it to avoid a crowded appearance.

Must you always single-space letters? Yes. Always? Well, almost always. If the letter is short and looks better double-spaced, then double-space it. If it contains questions you expect your correspondent to answer on the letter, double-space to give him room. As always, if you have good reason to break a rule, do so.

Understanding the Parts of a Letter

The parts of a business letter, which are described in detail in the remainder of this section, are identified in the model letter shown in exhibit D. Follow accepted practice in each part of your letter. Don't waste time trying to be creative with the long-established conventions that dictate the order, spacing, and content of letter parts.

EXHIBIT C. LETTER-PLACEMENT SCALE

For Elite Typewriter

Approximate Number of Words in Letter	Length of Line	Line Spaces from Top of Page to Inside Address	Line Spaces from Date to Inside Address (Letterhead Used)	Line Spaces from Top of Page to Heading (Letterhead Not Used)
Under 100	50	25	10	13
100 - 150	50	22	8	12
150 - 200	60	21	6	13
200 - 250	60	19	6	11
250 - 300	70	16	6	8
300 - 350	70	14	4	8
Over 350	Two-page letter			

For Pica Typewriter

Approximate Number of Words in Letter	Length of Line	Line Spaces from Top of Page to Inside Address	Line Spaces from Date to Inside Address (Letterhead Used)	Line Spaces from Top of Page to Heading (Letterhead Not Used)
Under 100	40	23	8	14
100 - 150	50	20	6	12
150 - 200	60	20	4	14
200 - 250	60	17	4	11
Over 250	Two-page letter			

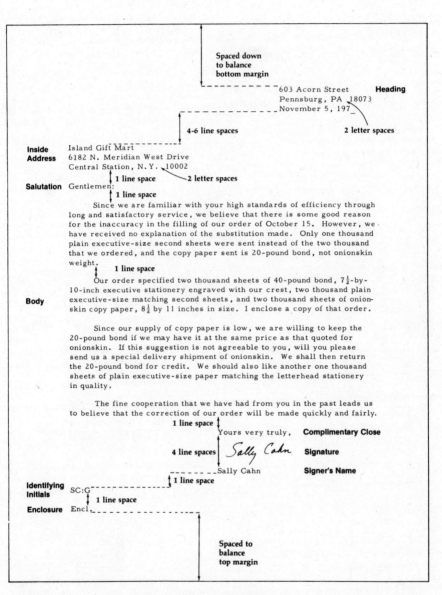

**Spaced down
to balance
bottom margin**

603 Acorn Street   **Heading**
Pennsburg, PA 18073
November 5, 197_

     4-6 line spaces   **2 letter spaces**

**Inside
Address**   Island Gift Mart
6182 N. Meridian West Drive
Central Station, N.Y. 10002

1 line space   **2 letter spaces**

Salutation   Gentlemen:

1 line space

Since we are familiar with your high standards of efficiency through
long and satisfactory service, we believe that there is some good reason
for the inaccuracy in the filling of our order of October 15. However, we
have received no explanation of the substitution made. Only one thousand
plain executive-size second sheets were sent instead of the two thousand
that we ordered, and the copy paper sent is 20-pound bond, not onionskin
weight.

1 line space

Our order specified two thousand sheets of 40-pound bond, $7\frac{1}{2}$-by-
10-inch executive stationery engraved with our crest, two thousand plain

Body   executive-size matching second sheets, and two thousand sheets of onionskin copy paper, $8\frac{1}{2}$ by 11 inches in size. I enclose a copy of that order.

Since our supply of copy paper is low, we are willing to keep the
20-pound bond if we may have it at the same price as that quoted for
onionskin. If this suggestion is not agreeable to you, will you please
send us a special delivery shipment of onionskin. We shall then return
the 20-pound bond for credit. We should also like another one thousand
sheets of plain executive-size paper matching the letterhead stationery
in quality.

The fine cooperation that we have had from you in the past leads us
to believe that the correction of our order will be made quickly and fairly.

1 line space

Yours very truly,   **Complimentary Close**

4 line spaces   *Sally Cahn*   **Signature**

Sally Cahn   **Signer's Name**

1 line space

**Identifying
Initials**   SC:G

1 line space

Enclosure   Encl.

**Spaced to
balance
top margin**

EXHIBIT D. SAMPLE LETTER SHOWING ESSENTIAL AND OCCASIONAL PARTS

Heading

The address of the writer and the date the letter is written make up the heading. On letterhead paper, only the date is written in. It may be centered on the line or placed at the left margin, the right margin, or some spot between the center of the line and the right margin. Spell out the name of the month in full; never abbreviate it.

If there is no printed letterhead on your writing paper, type your mailing address and the date in block style. No part of the heading should extend into the margin. The words *Street, Avenue, West,* and *East* are usually spelled in full, as are the names of states unless unbalanced lines result. Traditional abbreviations of state names or the newer two-letter abbreviations authorized for use with ZIP codes may be used. The ZIP code begins two spaces after the name of the state.

ABBREVIATIONS FOR NAMES OF STATES, TERRITORIES,
AND UNITED STATES POSSESSIONS

Alabama	Ala.	Nevada	Nev.
Arizona	Ariz.	New Hampshire	N. H.
Arkansas	Ark.	New Jersey	N. J.
California	Calif.	New Mexico	N. Mex.
Canal Zone	C. Z.	New York	N. Y.
Colorado	Colo.	North Carolina	N. C.
Connecticut	Conn.	North Dakota	N. Dak.
Delaware	Del.	Oklahoma	Okla.
District of Columbia	D. C.	Oregon	Oreg.
Florida	Fla.	Pennsylvania	Pa.
Georgia	Ga.	Philippine Islands	P. I.
Illinois	Ill.	Puerto Rico	P. R.
Indiana	Ind.	Rhode Island	R.I.
Kansas	Kans.	South Carolina	S. C.
Kentucky	Ky.	South Dakota	S. Dak.
Louisiana	La.	Tennessee	Tenn.
Maryland	Md.	Texas	Tex.
Massachusetts	Mass.	Vermont	Vt.
Michigan	Mich.	Virginia	Va.
Minnesota	Minn.	Washington	Wash.
Mississippi	Miss.	West Virginia	W. Va.
Missouri	Mo.	Wisconsin	Wis.
Montana	Mont.	Wyoming	Wyo.
Nebraska	Nebr.		

Do not abbreviate *Alaska, Hawaii, Iowa, Idaho, Maine, Ohio, Utah, Samoa, Guam,* or *Virgin Islands.*

UNITED STATES POSTAL SERVICE ABBREVIATIONS
FOR USE WITH ZIP CODE NUMBERS

Alabama	AL	Montana	MT
Alaska	AK	Nebraska	NB
Arizona	AZ	Nevada	NV
Arkansas	AR	New Hampshire	NH
California	CA	New Jersey	NJ
Colorado	CO	New Mexico	NM
Connecticut	CT	New York	NY
Delaware	DE	North Carolina	NC
District of Columbia	DC	North Dakota	ND
Florida	FL	Ohio	OH
Georgia	GA	Oklahoma	OK
Guam	GU	Oregon	OR
Hawaii	HI	Pennsylvania	PA
Idaho	ID	Puerto Rico	PR
Illinois	IL	Rhode Island	RI
Indiana	IN	South Carolina	SC
Iowa	IA	South Dakota	SD
Kansas	KS	Tennessee	TN
Kentucky	KY	Texas	TX
Louisiana	LA	Utah	UT
Maine	ME	Vermont	VT
Maryland	MD	Virginia	VA
Massachusetts	MA	Virgin Islands	VI
Michigan	MI	Washington	WA
Minnesota	MN	West Virginia	WV
Mississippi	MS	Wisconsin	WI
Missouri	MO	Wyoming	WY

In general, use abbreviations in addresses only if there is no other way to balance the lines.

FAULTY: 222 East Susquehanna Boulevard   [*Unbalanced*]
York, Penna.   17400

IMPROVED: 222 E. Susquehanna Blvd.
York, Pennsylvania   17400

FAULTY: 222 Pennsylvania Avenue, South West   [*Too long*]
Punxsutawney, Pennsylvania   15767

IMPROVED: 222 Pennsylvania Avenue, S.W.
Punxsutawney, PA   15767

Practice varies on writing the names of numbered streets. Numbers up to and including ten are usually spelled out. Street names that are one-word numbers are also usually spelled out in headings, but exceptions and combinations are permissible to balance lines and ease reading. If the street name is a number expressed in more than one word, you have a choice of writing it out or using figures. Follow local practice, or use whatever looks best.

> 222 Twelfth Avenue
> Ten Twelfth Avenue
> Ninth Avenue and Nineteenth Street
> Sixth Avenue at 41 Street

But always use figures for streets numbered higher than a hundred—that is, with three or more digits.

> 321 West 256 Street

Note that suffixes are no longer generally used with figures in a street name; *41 Street* and *256 Street* are preferred to *41st Street* and *256th Street*.

Inside Address

The name and mailing address of the person you are writing to are called the inside address. In most business letters, it is typed at the left margin at least four lines below the date. In more personal messages like invitations, condolences, and some letters to government officials, which are usually written on small stationery, the inside address is placed on the left margin several lines below the signature.

Writing an inside address seems easy enough. But there are a few pitfalls.

The inside address must not extend beyond the center of the page. The form should follow the form of the heading. Write firm names as they are used by the firm, including any abbreviations. Use other standard abbreviations as needed to achieve balance. Don't use the percentage sign (%) to indicate "in care of"; use *c/o* instead. Put an apartment or room number after the street name on the same line. As in the heading, type the zip code two spaces after the name of the state on the same line.

Copy the name and address of your correspondent exactly as you see it on the letter you are answering. Don't assume that he has made mistakes in spelling his name or address. There are strange names in the world. If your correspondent gives you

Pat Harrelson
101 Burrowes S.
College Station, Florida   32920

don't assume that Pat is a man; don't assume that Pat is a woman. Moreover, don't assume that *S.* means "Street"; it may also mean "South." Write what you see.

Use titles in inside addresses with particular care. People are likely to be sensitive about them. The following titles are most often encountered in business correspondence.

Mr.   For addressing a man.

Mr. George Rowland

Messrs.   For addressing two or more men. Often used to address members of a professional firm (not a business organization) composed of men.

Messrs. Jones and Hitchcock

Miss   For addressing an unmarried woman or a married woman who prefers to use her maiden name or a professional name.

Miss Eileen Fitzgerald
Miss Alice Tully
Miss Elizabeth Taylor

Mrs.   For addressing a married woman. Widows and divorcées often prefer this title.

Mrs. John Tubbs
Mrs. Elizabeth Tubbs

Don't address a wife by her husband's professional title.

NONSTANDARD: Mrs. Prof. John Tubbs

Ms.   For addressing a woman who has indicated her preference for it, a woman who has indicated no preference at all, or a woman whose marital status you do not know.

Ms. Gloria Steinem

Misses   For addressing two or more unmarried women.

Misses Patricia C. Narducci and Lois Eigabroadt

Mesdames   For addressing two or more married or unmarried women.

> Mesdames Stone and Myers

Esquire (Esq.)   For addressing a man of high social or business standing in England. Although infrequently used in the United States, the title occasionally appears on letters to lawyers. It follows the name.

> Daniel Mummaugh, Esquire
> Harold Lange, Esq.

Honorable (Hon.)   For addressing high officials in federal, state, and local government.

> The Honorable Harry Shirk
> The Honorable Mr. Shirk
> Hon. Harry Shirk

Reverend (Rev.)   For addressing ministers and priests of religious organizations.

> The Reverend Paul Eric
> The Reverend Dr. Troll
> Rev. O. Osgood Brown

Rabbi   For addressing a Jewish minister in the United States. Not abbreviated.

> Rabbi George Levy
> Rabbi Levy

Doctor (Dr.)   For addressing anyone who holds a doctor's degree. Abbreviate it when it is followed by a full name. Write it out when it is followed by a surname only.

> Dr. Jennifer Hill
> Doctor Hill

Professor (Prof.)   For addressing college teachers who hold professorial rank. You may abbreviate it before a full name in an address.

> Professor Lewis G. Jennings
> Prof. Lewis G. Jennings
> Professor Jennings

Sr. and Jr.   These abbreviations are, in effect, titles. They follow a full name and are separated from it by a comma.

> Dr. Paul R. Rosenblatt, Sr.
> Mr. Henry M. Narducci, Jr.

THE
UNIVERSITY OF WINNIPEG
PORTAGE & BALMORAL
WINNIPEG, MAN.   R3B 2E9
CANADA

How to Make Your Letters Attractive and Correct   **39**

Note that two titles of the same significance should not be used, either before a name or one preceding and the other following.

INCORRECT: Prof. Dr. Jennings
Mr. Harold Lange, Esquire
Dr. Jennifer Hill, M.D.

Company and business titles—*Manager, Credit Manager, Chairman of the Board,* and many others—follow the bearer's name. They may be typed on the same line or on the next line down, whichever is needed to achieve balanced lines.

Ms. Roberta Corcoran   Mr. J. V. Lynn, Manager
Manager, Sales Division   Market Research Division

A special problem of address arises if both husband and wife are doctors. There are several acceptable options. In any message primarily addressed to the husband, or in cases where the professional status of the wife is not a factor, use this form:

Dr. and Mrs. Jason Bright

For any message involving the professional status of both, but generated primarily in one or the other's professional area, use the following form:

Dr. Jason Bright and   Dr. Josephine Bright and
Dr. Josephine Bright   Dr. Jason Bright

For messages involving the professional status of both in which they share equally, use alphabetical order. For invitations or notices of all kinds, it may be advisable to send separate messages.

Military titles before full names are abbreviated, both for officers and for enlisted personnel. Retired military personnel are addressed the same as those on active duty except that their service designation and the abbreviation *Ret* or *(Ret.)* are used after full names.

CAPT John Jones, USN (Ret.)   Col Jane Jones, USA Ret

If your firm does business with the military, you will likely have to write to an officer. Note the absence of periods in the official abbreviations that follow and the lack of spacing in many of them.

RANK	ARMY	AIR FORCE	MARINE CORPS
General of the ———	Gen of Army	GenAF	
General	GEN/Gen	GEN	Gen
Lieutenant General	Lt Gen	LtGen	LtGen
Major General	Maj Gen	MajGen	MajGen
Brigadier General	Brig Gen	BGen	BrigGen
Colonel	COL/Col	Col	Col
Lieutenant Colonel	Lt Col	LtCol	LtCol
Major	MAJ/Maj	Maj	Maj
Captain	Capt	Capt	Capt
First Lieutenant	1st Lt	1stLt	1stLt
Second Lieutenant	2d Lt	2ndLt	2dLt

NAVY

Fleet Admiral	FADM
Admiral	ADM
Vice Admiral	VADM
Rear Admiral	RADM
Captain	CAPT
Commander	CDR
Lieutenant Commander	LCDR
Lieutenant	LT
Lieutenant (junior grade)	LTJG
Ensign	ENS

The naval rank of commodore was abolished in 1899 and restored only briefly during World War II. The title *Commodore,* never abbreviated, is a courtesy given to the president of a yacht club and the senior captain of a merchant fleet.

Salutation

The first line of the inside address determines the choice of salutation. If a person's name is mentioned there, the salutation should include that name (unless, of course, it is something like *The George Washington Tea Company*). The most common form of salutation is *Dear* plus the appropriate title, such as *Mr.,* and the person's last name. If a company name or department name is used as the first line of the inside address, the salutation should usually be *Gentlemen.* If it is a firm of women, you may use the conventional *Mesdames* if it does not make you sick. A more palatable choice might be *Ladies.*

Almost everyone today is aware of the problem of implied, albeit unintentional, sexism in writing. In English, the traditional use of masculine forms to name someone of unknown gender makes "sexism" almost unavoidable. So far, no one has come up with a sensible, comprehensive solution to the problem. Thus, when you are writing to a company, a box number, or some other hidden receiver, use *Gentlemen* as your salutation. Even when an attention line is used, calling the attention of a particular man or woman, you are still writing to the company and you should still use *Gentlemen* as your salutation. However, when you receive a letter from someone who does not indicate his or her sex, don't guess. Names can sometimes fool you. Television drama star Michael Learned is a woman. To avoid the possibility of looking foolish or offending someone, use the name exactly as the correspondent gives it. If you are answering a letter from someone who gives you only "Oscar Jones," you should write *Dear Oscar Jones*.

In all formal business correspondence, follow the salutation with a colon.

Dear Mrs. Miller:
Gentlemen:

In less formal letters—for example, a letter written to a business associate who is also a friend—a comma is generally used after the salutation. Using a friend's nickname is quite proper in such a letter, but his full name should be used in the inside address.

Mr. J. R. Miller
Plant Superintendent
Sutton Engineering Corp.
Bellefonte, PA   16823
Dear Jay,

Except for proper names and titles in salutations, capitalize only the first letter of the first word.

My dear Senator Jones:

Most military officers are referred to by rank in the salutation. For officers whose rank is given in two words, use the second in the salutation. Titles of rank are not abbreviated here.

Lieutenant Commander Priscilla Beech
Dear Commander Beech:

Warrant officers of all grades are referred to as *Mr.*, *Ms.*, *Miss*, or *Mrs.*

Chief Warrant Officer Charles Teng
Dear Mr. Teng:

Body of a Letter

Begin the body of your letter two lines below the salutation. Single-space the lines in a paragraph. Double-space between paragraphs. Avoid long paragraphs.

If you must break a word at the end of a line, check a dictionary for proper syllabication. But be aware that some words are more sensibly divided by pronunciation than by the derivations shown in dictionaries.

bureauc-racy, bureau-cratic
photog-raphy, photo-graphic

When writing is set into type and printed in books, American practice is to divide words by pronunciation; British practice is to divide them by derivation. However, you will never be "wrong" if you divide words in typewritten material according to the syllabication shown in a dictionary. (See section 34, "How to Break Words.")

If your letter is long and will not fit neatly on one page, do not continue it on the back of the page. Use a matching "second sheet," a page without a letterhead. At the top of the second sheet, type the name of the person or firm written to, the number of the page, and the date. Continue the message three lines below the identification data. Start at the left margin. Don't continue a message of fewer than three lines to a second page. See exhibit E for an example of a second-sheet format.

Avoid the old-fashioned convention of writing a final "paragraph" that is nothing more than a participial phrase.

Trusting this will meet with your approval,
Hoping to receive the favor of your reply soon,

```
Mr. William J. Mitchell          -3-          July 10, 19--

when repeated efforts to contact you have been ignored.  Now the
problem is a legal one.  And if we don't hear from you soon, we will
be forced to take drastic action.

                              Yours truly,

                              Carlton Hoblak
                              Carlton Hoblak

   CH:P
```

EXHIBIT E. SAMPLE SECOND SHEET OF A LETTER

And don't begin your final paragraph with "I remain. . . ." Both constructions are outdated.

Complimentary Close and Signature

Begin the complimentary close two spaces below the last line of the message and at the center or a little to the right of center of the page. In the full block format it begins on the left margin. In no case should it extend into a margin, right or left. Type the name four lines below the complimentary close.

Capitalize only the first word of a complimentary close. Use two words, not just *Sincerely* or *Cordially*, and follow the close with a comma.

For regular correspondence (considered a bit formal)	Very truly yours, Yours very truly, Yours truly,
For business acquaintances (increasingly popular for all but very formal contexts)	Sincerely yours, Yours sincerely, Very sincerely yours,
For formal letters to superiors	Respectfully yours,
For business friends	Cordially yours,

Signature and close in widespread use

Sincerely yours,

Harry Myers

Harry Myers

Signatures and closings used with a company name

Yours very truly,   Very truly yours,

CENTRAL CASTINGS COMPANY   STONE VALLEY VISUALS

Orville J. Freep   *Helen Weber*

Orville J. Freep   Helen Weber
Sales Manager

Sincerely yours,   Sincerely yours,

KOZAC SIGN COMPANY   KOZAC SIGN COMPANY

Sarah C. Kozac   *Sarah C. Kozac*

Sarah C. Kozac   President
President

You may arrange the complimentary close and signature block almost any way you want to balance the lines and achieve an attractive appearance.

Proofread everything you sign. The signature shows who has responsibility for the message. Write legibly in ink. The first name after the complimentary close has legal responsibility for the letter. If you want the company to have that responsibility, use its name after the close.

Very truly yours,

KOZAC SIGN COMPANY

Sarah C. Kozac

Sarah C. Kozac
President

If you accept responsibility, omit the company name. (This statement, of course, is an oversimplification. In many cases a company has responsibility even though the writer did not include the company name. And in other cases the individual has responsibility even though he used the company name.)

Don't create problems for those who must respond to your letters. You have no right to expect your reader to assume that you are a woman or to infer that you are a man. If you care that the distinction be made in correspondence to you, show your preference in the close. A man should not use *Mr.* with his signature, but placing it in front of his typed name below the signature will spare the person who must write him a reply any uncertainty:

Sincerely yours,

Lee Dombroski

Mr. Lee Dombroski

Similarly, a woman who wants to keep sexual and marital distinctions out of her signature should type the designation she prefers below it:

Sincerely yours,

Evelyn Watts

Ms. [Miss or Mrs.] Evelyn Watts

In the past an unmarried woman placed *Miss* in parentheses in front of her signature. A married woman used *Mrs.* before her signature, with her husband's name in parentheses beneath. Some women still prefer these forms. Others find these distinctions irksome.

A single or married woman who prefers to leave marital status out of her correspondence would use the *Ms.* variation of the basic form just shown:

Yours very truly,

Andrea Wilson

Ms. Andrea Wilson

A single woman who prefers to have her single status known would choose the *Miss* variation and type *Miss Andrea Wilson* below her signature. A married woman who wants her married status known would use the *Mrs.* variation. A single woman may prefer this form:

    Yours truly,

    (Miss) Jan Hetzel

    Jan Hetzel

A married woman who prefers to have her husband's name known by the reader may use this form:

    Yours truly,

    Mrs. Mildred Richards

    (Mrs. Henry Richards)

Widows may sign their correspondence in either of two ways:

Yours truly,	Yours truly,
Harriet K. Arnold	*(Mrs.) Harriet K. Arnold*
Harriet K. Arnold	Harriet K. Arnold
(Mrs. Horace Arnold)	

    Use either of the following forms when the secretary signs for the boss:

Very truly yours,	Very truly yours,
KOZAC SIGN COMPANY	KOZAC SIGN COMPANY
Sarah C. Kozac	*William Stein*
Sarah C. Kozac	Secretary to Sarah Kozac
by William Stein	

For accepted forms used in writing to specific civil, religious, and academic officials, see the appendix, "Additional Forms of Address, Salutation, and Complimentary Close."

Other Occasional Parts of a Letter

Attention line. Use an attention line in those few cases when the message of your letter is directed to the company but when you prefer that your business be handled by someone you have dealt with in the past if he is still there. You have several options for placing an attention line. You can locate it two lines below the inside address, flush with the margin or centered. Or you can place it on the same line as the salutation. However, don't place it below the salutation.

Ajax Biscuit Company 100 Norwood Drive Briggs, Texas 78608	Ajax Biscuit Company 100 Norwood Drive Briggs, Texas 78608
Attention: Mr. C. P. Long	Attention: Mr. C. P. Long
Gentlemen:	Gentlemen:

Ajax Biscuit Company
100 Norwood Drive
Briggs, Texas 78608

Gentlemen: Attention: Mr. C. P. Long

Subject line. The subject line identifies the subject of the message. Put it on the same line as the salutation or two lines below it. *Re* and *In re* are obsolete forms for announcing the subject.

Teletrix Corporation
320 West Scalp Street
Greensboro, GA 30642

Gentlemen: Subject: Memphis Caper 2000

The Plain Words Press
Box 198, R.D. 2
Eastport, N.Y. 11941

Gentlemen:

                               Subject: Student Group 530

Identifying initials. For later reference, all letters should have initials at the end to identify the dictator and the stenographer. Conventions vary widely from office to office. Both sets of initials are usually (but not always) typed in capital letters, the dictator's first and the stenographer's next, and are distinguished by the number of initials in each set. A colon, a dash, a slash, or an asterisk separates the two sets, typed solid with no extra space between. Some offices identify stenographers by number and some prefer the typist's initials to be below the dictator's. All the following formats are commonly used:

RGW:JK   PN—S   esm/rj   WGR*3   GRW
                                                      CPW

Whatever the format, put the identifying initials at the lower left margin on the same line as the typed name of the sender, or two lines below.

Enclosure. If any material other than the letter is to be mailed in the envelope, the word *Enclosure* is typed immediately below or two lines below the identifying initials, flush with the margin. The abbreviation *Enc.* or *Encl.* is often used. If more than one item is to be enclosed, indicate the number or list the items.

ASW:AE   ASW:AE   RW/T   JRM—EL
Enclosure
                 Enc.   Encl. 2   Enclosures: Photograph
                                                         Contract

Indications for carbon copies. Write *Copy to* or *cc* and the name of anyone who will receive a copy of the letter immediately below or two lines below the indication of the enclosure.

LTD:TH   SMG/WE
Enc.
cc: Harry Carter   Enclosure
     Susan Ritnor
                                   Copy to: Albert Fritz

If no items are to be enclosed, place the carbon copy indication below the identifying initials.

ER/S   TRY:PK
Copy to: Sam Shade   cc: Mildred Schick

Postscript. Since the last position in a piece of writing is a position of emphasis, a letter writer will sometimes use a postscript to stress an important point or elaborate a special consideration. To indicate a postscript, place the letters *P.S.* two lines below the identifying initials or two lines below the last notations and begin the message on the same line.

ASW/AL

P.S.   The widget may be returned at any time up to sixty days for a full refund.

Common Forms of Business Letters

Exhibits F–H show examples of the various formats you may use to arrange your letter on the page. Choose one you feel comfortable with or use the one that is standard in your office. Whatever your choice, use it consistently throughout the letter. Occasionally, you might see flamboyant departures from accepted formats, usually in sales letters. In these cases, the writer hopes the appearance of the letter will capture the reader's attention long enough to involve him in the message. Be wary of using extreme formats, however. An accepted format is almost always preferable. Because your reader is familiar with it, a standard format will guide him, without distraction, to the point of your letter.

Industrial Historians Inc.

PENNSBURG, PENNSYLVANIA

November 5, 19__

Island Gift Mart
6182 N. Meridian West Drive
Central Station, N.Y. 10002

Gentlemen:

Since we are familiar with your high standards of efficiency through long
and satisfactory service, we believe that there is some good reason for
the inaccuracy in the filling of our order of October 15. However, we
have received no explanation of the substitution made. Only one thousand
plain executive-size second sheets were sent instead of the two thousand
that we ordered, and the copy paper sent is 20-pound bond, not onionskin
weight.

Our order specified two thousand sheets of 40-pound bond, $7\frac{1}{2}$-by-10-inch
executive stationery engraved with our crest, two thousand plain executive-size matching second sheets, and two thousand sheets of onionskin
copy paper, $8\frac{1}{2}$ by 11 inches in size.

Since our supply of copy paper is low, we are willing to keep the 20-pound
bond if we may have it at the same price as that quoted for onionskin. If
this suggestion is not agreeable to you, will you please send us a special
delivery shipment of onionskin. We shall then return the 20-pound for
credit. We should also like another one thousand sheets of plain executive-size paper matching the letterhead stationery in quality.

The fine cooperation that we have had from you in the past leads us to
believe that the correction of our order will be made quickly and fairly.

Yours very truly,

Sally Cahn
President

SC:G

EXHIBIT F. SAMPLE LETTER IN FULL OR STRICT BLOCK STYLE

Industrial Historians Inc.
PENNSBURG, PENNSYLVANIA

November 5, 19__

Island Gift Mart
6182 N. Meridian West Drive
Central Station, N.Y. 10002

Gentlemen:

Since we are familiar with your high standards of efficiency through long
and satisfactory service, we believe that there is some good reason for
the inaccuracy in the filling of our order of October 15. However, we
have received no explanation of the substitution made. Only one thousand
plain executive-size second sheets were sent instead of the two thousand
that we ordered, and the copy paper sent is 20-pound bond, not onionskin
weight.

Our order specified two thousand sheets of 40-pound bond, $7\frac{1}{2}$-by-10-inch
executive stationery engraved with our crest, two thousand plain executive-size matching second sheets, and two thousand sheets of onionskin
copy paper, $8\frac{1}{2}$ by 11 inches in size. I enclose a copy of that order.

Since our supply of copy paper is low, we are willing to keep the 20-pound
bond if we may have it at the same price as that quoted for onionskin. If
this suggestion is not agreeable to you, will you please send us a special
delivery shipment of onionskin. We shall then return the 20-pound for
credit. We should also like another one thousand sheets of plain executive-size paper matching the letterhead stationery in quality.

The fine cooperation that we have had from you in the past leads us to
believe that the correction of our order will be made quickly and fairly.

Yours very truly,

INDUSTRIAL HISTORIANS INC.

Sally Cahn
President

SC:G

Enc.

**EXHIBIT G. SAMPLE LETTER IN FULL OR STRICT BLOCK STYLE WITH DATE,
COMPLIMENTARY CLOSE, AND SIGNATURE CENTERED**

Industrial Historians Inc.
PENNSBURG, PENNSYLVANIA

November 5, 19___

Island Gift Mart
6182 N. Meridian West Drive
Central Station, N.Y. 10002

Attention: Mrs. Jane Sorenz

Gentlemen:

Since we are familiar with your high standards of efficiency through long and satisfactory service, we believe that there is some good reason for the inaccuracy in the filling of our order of October 15. However, we have received no explanation of the substitution made. Only one thousand plain executive-size second sheets were sent instead of the two thousand that we ordered, and the copy paper sent is 20-pound bond, not onionskin weight.

Our order specified two thousand sheets of 40-pound bond, $7\frac{1}{2}$-by-10-inch executive stationery engraved with our crest, two thousand plain executive-size matching second sheets, and two thousand sheets of onion-skin copy paper, $8\frac{1}{2}$ by 11 inches in size.

Since our supply of copy paper is low, we are willing to keep the 20-pound bond if we may have it at the same price as that quoted for onionskin. If this suggestion is not agreeable to you, will you please send us a special delivery shipment of onionskin. We shall then return the 20-pound bond for credit. We should also like another one thousand sheets of plain executive-size paper matching the letterhead stationery in quality.

The fine cooperation that we have had from you in the past leads us to believe that the correction of our order will be made quickly and fairly.

Yours very truly,

Sally Cahn
President

SC:G

EXHIBIT H. SAMPLE LETTER IN SEMIBLOCK STYLE

Part Two

HOW TO WRITE REPORTS

How to Get in the Right Frame of Mind

The most widely heard criticism of the reports generated by the offices of government and industry is that they are unreadable. Ninety percent of the unreadable reports start to go bad before the writer ever picks up his pencil, for most writers of incomprehensible reports are doing the report for the wrong reasons. To avoid writing such a report, you must get in the right frame of mind.

Do Not Take an Ego Trip

Perhaps the most pernicious problem with reports in general is that the writer forgets the purpose of the report. In the ego trip report, instead of communicating information, the writer uses the report as a vehicle to sell himself. He tries to impress rather than inform. He uses long, involuted sentences. He is afraid a short word won't look as dazzling as a long one, so he says *manipulandum* instead of *lever*. He fills the report with the jargon of his trade so it won't sound "ordinary." He makes the report ten pages longer than it need be so it will "look" complete and thorough. He becomes quite proud of its heft and appearance. Unfortunately, such a report is rarely, if ever, written for the reader. It is written for the writer himself. An ego trip may make the writer feel important, but it makes pretty hard reading. The reader must spend twice the time it should take to winnow the information from the debris. He must unravel the tangled clauses, translate the jargon into everyday language, seek out the vital facts amid the elaborations. He gets tired, he gets bored, and finally he gets mad. Looking for shortcuts, he scans the pages, flips to the recommendations, and eventually gives up in disgust. Those extra ten pages, as well as a lot of others, remain unread. Reports written for the glorification of the writer end up being read by him alone.

How do you avoid the ego trip report? Turn the same psychology that urges you to write that type of report to your advantage. Remember some basic facts of human nature. People do not read reports to discover how wonderful the writer is. They commission and read reports because they need information. They want to get that information as quickly as possible. They value their time and, thus, will value you if you can save them time. So get to the point quickly; make your reports easy to read by keeping them as uncomplicated as possible. Do everything you can think of to help the reader get through the essential information in the shortest possible time. Write for the reader, not for yourself. You will end up serving yourself better with a brief, clear report. By all means, avoid windy, overcomplicated reports, but beware the other extreme; brevity can also be overdone.

Do Not Make a Chinese Puzzle

The writer of the Chinese puzzle report occasionally starts off with the right intention—to save the reader time—but gets so carried away he defeats his own purpose. More often, he wishes he didn't have to do the report at all—and every line shows it. Whatever the motivation, each writer ends up giving the impression that he was concerned primarily with saving his own time. His sentences are short; his style telegraphic; his paragraphs too brief to show logical connections from one idea to the next. Transition paragraphs are eliminated entirely. Sometimes helpful sections of the report are omitted, such as a section on the way the report is organized if the reader needs guidance through an unusual method of presentation. This cryptic writer doesn't bother to prepare the reader for upcoming tables, charts, or graphs, or, having presented them, neglects to indicate what point should be drawn from them. Sometimes he relies heavily on the imperative sentence and ends up sounding curt. In addition, he may put essential information in an appendix, thus forcing his increasingly weary reader to flip back and forth throughout the text to figure out what's going on. The reader will resent what seems to him to be a mass of raw, unexplained data dumped in his lap. If you make the mistake of writing a Chinese puzzle report, it will seem to the reader that you have submitted your notes rather than the finished report. He will see your report as incomplete, disorganized, and illogical, and think of you as lazy.

Be Brief, Clear, and Complete

If you are worried that your effort to be brief might be resulting in a cryptic report, by all means show it to someone else. A word of caution here: Choose someone because he is qualified to tell you what you need to know to improve the report, not because he will tell you what you want to hear. It is infinitely more desirable to have a disinterested third party find fault with your rough draft than to end up having your employer dissatisfied with the finished product. In addition, bear in mind that a report is too long only if it is longer than it needs to be. A rather short report may be too long if it could have told the reader all he needs to know more quickly. Similarly, thick reports can be incomplete if they fail to include necessary information. The criterion is not the number of pages but how helpful the writer has been in reporting, clarifying, and interpreting. As you can see, your job includes more than just recording the data; you must show the reader what the data mean.

SECTION 8

How to Make Your Report Effective

Now that you know that a wrong attitude can derail your report, let's look at some rules that will keep you on the right track.

Keep the Reader in Mind at All Times

To have value your report must be read and understood. As you write, become the reader as well as the writer. Put yourself in his place. Imagine him reading every word over your shoulder. Never forget he's there. The report is *for him*. The reader, of course, can be your employer, a committee, the board of directors, or members of an organization—one or many people. Your very first job as writer should be to *research the reader*. Find out all you can about what he wants, what he will need to know to understand your report and follow your recommendation.

Organize Everything

By the time you get to the actual writing stage (see section 9, "How to Get Organized"), you will know your material inside out. Naturally you cannot hope to write a comprehensive report without being totally familiar with your data. However, knowing the subject well does not necessarily mean you will write about it well unless you observe a few precautions.

Don't Try to Say It All at Once

For example, if you are working on the introduction, avoid the ever present temptation to draw conclusions there. Longfellow's advice "Each thing in its place is best" is a good guideline to follow. Keep introductory materials in the introductory sections and recommendations in the recommendations section. Parts of the report must be treated in sequence. Adopt a logical method of presentation and stick to it. If you have announced in the title of a section that you will discuss methods you used to gather data, don't report the data themselves there. Sound obvious? You'd be surprised to find how often that obvious rule is violated.

Explain Each Point You Make

The report must be developed within each section, that is, with paragraphs in which elements of the controlling idea are expressed, demonstrated, and validated. Tell *why* you did the things you did. *Explain* the procedures you used: tell *what* information you were after and what you hoped to achieve by using the methods you chose. Developed paragraphs unfold before the reader the specifics he needs to understand and accept your point.

Support General Statements

No employer worth his job will move his plant to Albuquerque just because you say he should. Yet the report writer who does not supply the reader with specific facts and details to validate each point, conclusion, method, or procedure is in effect asking his employer to act on the writer's word alone. No one with decision-making power can long afford to be so naive as to make choices on faith. Your report will be a waste of his time if it is too general; he will not be able to see your logic or evaluate your results.

Use Specifics

The reader will need lots of detailed information from carefully chosen and documented sources. He will need to know that you checked everything thoroughly. It will not be enough for you to assure him that you did. You must *show* him you did by giving him the *facts*. Saying your report is comprehensive does not make it so. Use specifics to demonstrate its validity. For example, if you found the following excerpts from two reports on the same topic, which writer would you believe did a complete job?

> WRITER 1: I checked the number of competing brands of acne remedies in several stores throughout the city.
>
> WRITER 2: To get some idea of the number of competing cleansing formulas being marketed locally, I made an informal survey on March 3, 197–, of acne remedies on display at Aid-You Drugs and Self-Patch Drug Store, both in downtown Xanadu.

Notice in the first example that you can only guess about what the writer did and why he wanted to do it in the first place. How extensive was his survey? Writer 1 gives no clue. How many stores? Which ones? Notice how the use of specifics by writer 2 lends support to his methods and inspires confidence in his work. Writer 1 leaves too much guesswork to the reader. You cannot evaluate the worth of the survey. Thus, as presented by writer 1, the survey was worthless.

Use Meaningful Sentence Structure

Sometimes valid reports are ignored because the writer does not demonstrate his intentions and his logic consistently throughout the paper. Remembering that your job is to do everything you can to help the reader, you will want to guide him carefully through the development of your point by using sentence phrasing that reflects your logic. You will want to use *signpost words* that signal logical development—words such as *therefore, however, thus, nonetheless, nevertheless,* and *in addition*. You will also want to combine related thoughts into a meaningful, economic statement. Instead of writing

> I constructed a questionnaire of five items. I questioned twenty-five customers as they left each drugstore. These interviews were done on March 14. Below is a copy of the questionnaire.

you will try to show relationships and significance by rephrasing:

> On March 14, I used the following five-item questionnaire to interview twenty-five customers from each drugstore.

In addition, you will be alert to the advantages of subordinating less critical thoughts to weightier ones within sentences by pointing out relationships grammatically. You could, for example, write

> Racial tensions in our prisons are a serious problem. I traveled to twenty-five states interviewing a total of thirty-four wardens to get their views.

Putting yourself in the reader's place, notice the difficult time he has trying to figure out how the second sentence supports the general statement in the first sentence. What *is* the writer's logic? What does he mean? Is he saying

> Since racial tensions in our prisons are such a serious problem, I interviewed thirty-four wardens in twenty-five states to get a comprehensive look at the problem from their viewpoint.

or did he mean

> Even though racial tensions in our prisons are a serious problem, I interviewed thirty-four wardens in twenty-five states to get their views on a number of current crises in our penal system.

Or does he, in fact, mean something else quite different? The writer is charged with saying what he means; it is not the reader's problem to conjure the logic from truths veiled by a murky text. Use the tools at hand to point out the way to the reader. He will react instinctively to signpost words, to sentence structure that subordinates less important thoughts as a method of clarifying and highlighting major ones. He will feel secure when he sees details and specifics.

How to Get Organized

You can't deliver your information all at once. You must say some things before you say others. The order in which you present your thoughts is organization. It is determined by the nature of the subject and your judgment of the needs of the reader.

Getting Started

There is no formula that will enable you to know quickly the ideal sequence for every piece of writing. But if you are stuck, a review of the following options may get you going.

Time Order

If your material is a narrative of events or directions for doing something, time order is inescapable. First this happened, then that happened, and so on, until the end.

> In the GT finale, Trans-Am regular Warren Agor got his Camaro in front at the start and led for the first 30 laps. (Agor had started the first 100-miler thirty-first, the result of a blown engine in practice which forced him to qualify via a consolation race.) Gregg, who was never more than a few car lengths behind Agor, finally got his Carrera past the big orange Camaro, in a heavy traffic situation, and held the lead until the finish. Posey maintained third place. Keyser dropped to fourth, but earned enough points to keep him ahead of Gregg in the Camel GT drivers' championship.

Or, first you do this and then you do that.

> To make old-fashioned cottage cheese, heat very slowly one quart unpasteurized naturally sour skim milk in a double boiler. Put in strainer lined with cheese cloth and drain. Rinse with about a quart of warm

water and repeat rinsing two more times. Let drain until curd is free of
whey. Moisten with cream and salt to taste.

Space Order

This is the natural order for description. You tell where things are in
relationship to each other and to fixed points outside.

> Huntingdon County, an area of 918 square miles or 587,520 acres, is
> situated in south-central Pennsylvania. This is a section of long, narrow
> valleys, separated or shut in on all sides by long, narrow, steep, rugged
> mountain ranges that parallel one another for many miles in a northeast-
> southwest direction. Nearly all of the county is drained by the Juniata
> River, which rises at the foot of the Allegheny Mountains escarpment to
> the west, flows in a general southeasterly direction through the moun-
> tains and across the valleys of the central part, and thence flows east-
> ward to the Susquehanna River. The Juniata River has provided a natu-
> ral east-west passageway from one valley to another by cutting deep
> gaps in the mountain ranges.
>
> The extreme north-south length of the county is about 48 miles; the
> east-west width ranges from about thirteen miles at the narrowest point
> to more than thirty miles at the widest point, which is from the top of
> Tussey Mountain near Saxton to Tuscarora Mountain near Blairs Mills.

Simple to Complex Order

When dealing with a frustration of complexity, start with the simplest,
the easiest. When that is clarified, go to the next easiest. Conquer the
whole by conquering the parts in the order of their simplicity. This is
the natural order for any attempt to explain a mechanism. In an essay
on why an airplane flies, Wolfgang Langewiesche starts with the simplest idea, the shape of the wing. This has to be understood first, since
the underlying principle of the device resides in the shape of the
wing. He then goes on to "thrust" and "drag," dividing these complex
factors into parts and finding simple terms to analyze them.

Familiar to Unfamiliar Order

Some material can be handled by arranging its parts according to the
reader's probable degree of familiarity with each part. If you start with
the most familiar, the analysis of the least familiar will be easier to understand by the time you get to it.

Choosing a Method of Presentation

If you are fortunate, your company will have a manual showing its preferences for the format and style of reports. Maybe you've been lucky enough to obtain earlier reports to study how others handled the problems of presentation and organization. Make sure, though, that you've chosen as your model a report that is valued by the people who will read yours.

Perhaps you're unlucky. No style manual, no decent reports on file. What then? Here are some things you ought to try before you decide to revolutionize singlehandedly the art of report writing:

1. Many professional organizations put out style manuals. Even if you are not a member, most of these organizations will gladly supply you with pertinent publications for a reasonable fee. Try them.
2. Don't forget your local bookstore and the public library. A helpful clerk or librarian should be able to supply you with numerous guides to style and format.

If the office you work for does not prescribe an arrangement of material in reports, you might profit from looking at the following sequences taken from company manuals:

Introduction
  a. Statement of problem
  b. Importance of solving
    the problem
Analysis
Conclusions
Recommendations

Conclusions and Recommendations
Introduction
Procedure
Discussion of Results
Future Plans
  Appendix

Introduction
Procedure and Results
Conclusions and Recommendations
Experimental Section

If you have to make a progress report, the following outline may help you solve the problem of choosing a sensible method of organizing your material:

Introduction
   a. Statement of problem
   b. Scope
   c. Method of investigation
Present Status of Investigation
Progress to Date
Work to Be Done
Forecast

On the basis of the position of conclusions and recommendations, reports are classified into two categories: conclusions and recommendations first and conclusions and recommendations last. Conclusions first makes for a slightly more compact, more economical, more readable report since the reader knows the result immediately. Conclusions first is recommended for material that is not likely to be controversial. If the material is controversial, that is, if the conclusion or recommendation is likely to make the reader angry, cause great resentment, or in other ways prejudice the reader against the argument, it is better to use the logical order embodied in the following questions:

What is the problem?
What did I do to solve it?
What did I find?
What does my discovery mean?
What should we do now?

The conclusion will be more acceptable if the argument and logical structures precede it. The following are some typical outlines using logical (conclusions last) order:

Introduction	Introduction
Summary of Problem	Present Method
Discussion	Proposed Method
Suggested Solution	Conclusions and Recommendations
Conclusions	

Introduction
Presentation of Facts and Analysis
Conclusions and Recommendations

These are some typical outlines using psychological (conclusions first) order:

Synopsis	Introduction
Introduction	Summation Section
Conclusions and Recommendations	Technical Section
Experimental Procedure	Visual Aid Section
Results and Analysis	Supplementary Section
Appendix	

Conclusions
Introduction
Discussion
Summary
Computations and Other Exhibits

Recommendations	Statement of Problem
Conclusions	Procedure
Explanation of the Problem	Recommendation
Summary	Conclusions
	Facts Supporting Conclusions (Rationale)
	Appendix

Whichever format you finally choose, you should know that they all are evolved from a single premise: consistency. The report that follows a consistent format helps the reader; he learns quickly what to expect. Don't surprise him; he will only become confused. Choose the format and style that suit your purposes and material best and stick with them. Don't, for instance, suddenly decide to change the appearance of your major headings from lower-case letters to all capitals halfway through your report. The reader will not know why you changed your mind. He won't understand what's going on. The report will begin to seem inconsistent and, eventually, illogical to him. (You'll either have to go back and change those in the first half or stay with the lower-case letters.) Suggestion: Have someone with a sharp eye for detail proofread your report, looking specifically for inconsistencies in format and style. Try to choose someone other than the person you've chosen to read your report for content.

Making a Rough Draft

If the sight of the blank page seems to paralyze you, if you don't know where or how to begin, don't worry. You are not alone. Such doubts and hesitations are universal, and they are all to the good. They will force you to experiment, to search for the best way to make a point, organize a section, and display your data. Clear writing takes time, patience, and a willingness to refine, reorganize, reduce, and recast your first notes many times before crisp sentences take shape and the inevitable logic of the report itself unfolds. The progression will move from thought to sentence to paragraph to section—until finally you have a report. If you sit down with the idea "Tonight I am going to write that report," you are doomed to a night with a full wastebasket and an empty coffee pot. Think small. Say to yourself, "Tonight I am going to jot down everything I can think of that might belong in the introduction." Or perhaps you can be even more restricted, and write down everything that ought to go in the procedures section of the introduction.

If talking has always been your most effective means of communicating, there is no need to abandon it just because you are writing a report. Try dictating to obtain a first draft (see section 21, "How to Dictate").

Whether you write or dictate, first organize your material into three broad categories generally corresponding to introduction, body, and conclusions. Then, starting with the introduction, or preferably a section of the introduction, try to tell the reader what you are doing and why. Don't worry at this point about being clever or neat or grammatical or organized. Feel free to be slapdash. Jot down whatever occurs to you. Just try to get it all down—don't make judgments yet about whether or not it belongs, or even if it makes much sense. You'll have plenty of time later to cut and fit, polish and preen. One more thing: Don't throw away rough drafts. You never know when you might want to restore something that you have cut out.

SECTION 10

How to Set Up a Full-Dress Report

A "full-dress" report can have as many as a dozen or more parts, but you may not need all of them to write a complete report. Use only as many of the parts as your material and assignment require. In general, work at scaling down the final product if you can. Always remember that someone is going to have to read your report, so drop sections that aren't absolutely necessary and consider combining others to cut length and tighten organization.

Cover Page

You will need a cover page when you have a letter of authorization and choose to locate it before the title page. The cover page protects the letter and identifies the subject and author of the report. Do not confuse this page with a folder or binder that you may want to use for additional protection of the entire report. The complete title, if not too long, or the title in brief form, along with the author's name, should be well spaced on the cover page. Since the actual counting of report pages begins with the title page, the cover page is not counted.

Letter of Authorization

The letter of authorization shows the reader the assignment you were given. This letter is from your sponsor, the person who authorized you to undertake the report. Naturally, then, it can be included only if you received such a letter. Normally the letter makes the assignment and explains the problem, telling you what is to be done and why. Since the letter was not written by the report writer, some prefer to illustrate that distinction by locating the letter before the title page. Others find it more convenient to place it after the title page, thus eliminating the need for a cover page.

Since it is a letter, the authorization page is neither titled nor numbered. That is, it should look like a letter suitable for mailing and not like a page from a report. The letter is counted if it appears after the title page, but not counted when it appears before the title page.

Title Page

The title page tells the reader what the report is about (title), for whom it was written (name and title of sponsor), who wrote it (name and title of writer), and where and when it was written (place and date). In most cases it will be the first page of the report.

The title of your report should be concise—try for under twenty words—and at the same time specific. Thus you must make every word count to avoid being too general or too windy. Avoid introducing the title with obvious, and hence wasteful, phrases like *A Report on* or *A Survey of*. Get to the point quickly in your title, as well as throughout the report. Be as specific as you can be. Take a look at the evolution the following title went through:

> FIRST TRY: Should Mom's Away Nursery Schools Open a School in State College, Pennsylvania?

You already know by the time you write the report whether or not State College is a good location. The reader wants to know too. Unless you have a good reason, don't act as if you're writing a whodunit. Don't tease the reader. Some good reasons for a title that holds off the answer until the end of the report might include the following: (1) if your reader has some objections to, or preconceptions about, State College that you hope to overcome in the report; (2) if the evidence is not at all clear-cut—pros and cons balance out—and you thus recommend further study.

> SECOND TRY: Mom's Away Nursery Schools Ought to Consider Opening a School in State College, Pennsylvania

The emphasis here is on Mom's Away and not on the location that the study is about. In addition, *ought to consider* is imprecise and weak.

> FINAL TITLE: State College, Pennsylvania: An Excellent Location for a Mom's Away Nursery School

Space information on the title page to effect a balanced, visually attractive, and easily read presentation. Actual report numbering begins here, but no number appears on this page. In other words, the title page is counted as page i (lower-case roman numbers indicate all those pages that precede the text of the report), but you don't put the number on the page. Doing so would be to state the obvious.

Feel free to vary the format as it suits your needs and purposes. You may, for example, wish to put the names of your and your sponsor's organizations under your respective titles. Avoid complicated or showy arrangements, however. You don't need graphic gimmicks to attract attention. Keep your title page simple, dignified, and professional in appearance and layout. See exhibit I for an example.

State College, Pennsylvania:

An Excellent Location for a Mom's Away Nursery School

prepared for

Teresa Dolan, President

Mom's Away Nursery Schools

prepared by

Wilson Cooke, Assistant

Market Research Department

Philadelphia, Pennsylvania

August 12, 19--

EXHIBIT I. SAMPLE TITLE PAGE

Letter of Transmittal

The letter of transmittal, written by the author of the report, is used for reports to a specific sponsor or organization. A preface is substituted for the letter in those reports written for a large and widespread number of readers, such as a public affairs report. The letter *transmits* the report and refers to the *authorization*.

> Here is the report [transmittal function] you asked me to do on August 17, 19— [authorization function].

The letter should also include a brief *statement of the problem,* or explanation of the job you were assigned in the report.

> As you recall, you asked me to conduct an in-depth representative survey of nonunion members at the Jolliet plant to discover how these workers compared themselves to their unionized co-workers.

(You might want to give more details here, depending on the amount of detail in the presentation of the original assignment.) The letter traditionally ends with a positive indication of *appreciation* and *offer of future help.*

> Since I am involved with labor negotiations here at the St. Paul office, I was grateful for the chance to learn more about nonunion members and their attitudes about themselves and others. If you need any additional information or have a problem you think I can help you with, you can reach me at the office (277-9214) or at home (772-9160).

Your letter may also include any, but usually not all, of the following:

1. *Brief summary of results.*
2. *Acknowledgments of special help.* Remember here that the letter is to your sponsor and not to the person to whom you are indebted. It would be inappropriate phrasing to say, "I would like to thank John Volume, Head Bibliographer, Seattle Public Library." To thank Mr. Volume you'll have to tell him directly yourself. You can say properly, however, "John Volume, Head Bibliographer, Seattle Public Library, was most helpful in supplying me with necessary information for this report."

3. *An explanation of the general organization of the report,* especially if your organization is uncommon.
4. *Any interesting sidelights* to your study that you think the reader would like to know.
5. *Mention of any unusual experience* you had or any helpful facts you discovered in preparing the report that do not appear in the text.
6. *Announcement of your conclusions and recommendations* with a few major supporting reasons. Your letter would not include this item when you are using conclusions last organization in the report. You would have chosen that method because your conclusions are controversial or are supported by intricate data that must be carefully laid out in advance. Thus, to reveal conclusions in the letter would defeat your logic for organizing the report in the way you have done.
7. *Brief explanation of your procedures or methods.*
8. *Mention of limitations to the report* or any problems you encountered. Be careful here not to let the letter sound like an apology for the report that follows. If you did have troubles, let your sentences emphasize the steps you took to overcome them. Legitimate explanations of limitations to your study or research are valuable. State them completely but don't dwell on them. Leave the reader with the impression that, problems notwithstanding, you have done a thorough and competent job with the material and time available to you.

In deciding whether you should use any of the above in your letter, be guided by two rules of thumb. First, keep the length of the letter down to one page. If you find that it will go on to a second page, get out the blue pencil and use it wherever possible to cut out anything that isn't absolutely vital. Second, make sure that the letter contains everything the reader will need to know to understand the report. Tell him in the letter of transmittal those things you would tell him face to face when handing him the report.

The letter should look like a letter suitable for mailing (inside address, salutation, complimentary close, and so on—see exhibit J). It is counted as page ii of the report (page iii if letter of authorization is used after the title page) but, since it is a letter, the number usually does not appear on the page. Don't forget to sign the letter.

Mom's Away, Inc. Tranquility, N.J. 07879

August 12, 19--

Ms. Teresa Dolan
Mom's Away Nursery Schools
7125 Center City Square
Philadelphia, PA 19151

Dear Ms. Dolan:

Here is the report you asked me to do on July 1, 19--, to determine if State College, Pennsylvania, is a suitable location for a Mom's Away Nursery School.

State College looks like an ideal place for one of our schools. Only three schools are presently operating in the area, serving but 3 percent of the children of nursery school age. Our interviews with two hundred randomly chosen families having three- to five-year-old children add further support. An incredible 72 percent agreed they would use the school either full or part time, even if prices were slightly higher than those at other area nursery schools. Significantly, 37 percent asked to be put on a waiting list should the school open within the next year. Local ordinances and zoning requirements harmonize with Mom's Away's emphasis on attractive, well-planned physical plants. Because of the community's need for our services and Mom's Away's fine reputation, officials we talked with are hopeful Mom's will choose to locate in State College. For these reasons, I recommend that you go ahead with the financial analysis and site location study for State College.

My assistants, Dolores Glick and Natalie DeLuca, and I thoroughly enjoyed our three weeks researching the study. We are excited about the prospect of establishing a Mom's Away Nursery School in State College.

If you have any questions or need further help, please call me at the office or at home (328-6970).

Sincerely yours,

Wilson Cooke

Wilson Cooke, Assistant
Market Research

EXHIBIT J. SAMPLE LETTER OF TRANSMITTAL

Table of Contents

The table of contents, often labeled simply *Contents*, tells the reader what is included in the report and where to find it. It is also in both function and appearance a heading outline of the report itself. For this reason, scrupulous attention to the content and format of the table of contents will pay off in a logically organized report. Write the table of contents after you have a rough draft of the report. Study it closely to make sure it conforms to the rules for effective, logical headings. Read section 11, "How to Use Headings," to be certain you have it right.

The contents page is marked iii (or iv with authorization letter after title page) and is the first to have the number typed on the page. Center the number at the bottom and title the page *Contents,* or *Table of Contents,* at the top center. The page should look neat and un-crowded. Avoid crowding between headings or leaving too large a margin at the bottom. Center information on the page. Use spaced periods from the end of each heading to its corresponding page number. See exhibit K for an example of a contents page.

What should you include in the table of contents? Do not list the title page or the table itself. Presumably the reader can find the title page without directions. And he'll know where the contents are because he will be looking at them. You may begin with the letters of authorization and transmittal if you wish. If your table is short, include them. If including them will give the page a crowded appearance or force you on to another page, then don't. Should you decide to list the letters, place them at the left-hand margin like your major, or first-level, headings. Second-level headings should be indented and look different from major headings in both the table of contents and the text. The reader should be able to see the organizational relationship of the headings at a glance. Third-level headings appear in the text, but usually not in the table, since including them would take up too much space. They too should look substantially different from first- and second-level headings. You can achieve this different look with the use of indentation, spacing, capitalization, underlining, italics, colors, and so on. To be sure your reader can follow along, it is best to use a combination of these aids. If you cannot make all heading levels visually distinctive, use actual numbering and letters.

The bibliography, if there is one, is listed at the end of the report outline and, like the letters, is placed flush against the left margin. Make your major, first-level headings, through capitalization or un-derlining, clearly the most imposing items on the page. Indicate typo-

Contents

iv

EXHIBIT K. SAMPLE TABLE OF CONTENTS

graphically that the listed letters and bibliography are not so important.

If you have any appendix material, each brochure, chart, or graph should be named individually. You can do it like this:

List appendix items by name, in consecutive order, continuing your numbering of them from the last page of actual text throughout the appendix pieces. Usually you can avoid using the word *Appendix* in the contents. The title of each item you give in the contents should correspond exactly to the way the title appears on its respective page.

List of Tables, List of Charts, List of Illustrations

A list of tables is particularly useful in those reports that rely heavily on charted and illustrated data, particularly scientific and figure analysis reports (see section 12, "How to Use Charts, Tables, and Lists"). If you have many—say, over five—charts, graphs, or tables, you may want to consider listing them separately, with their respective page numbers, on a page following the table of contents. You can list tables first, then charts if you have both. Label each list carefully so the reader knows what he's reading. For example, if you have five tables and nine charts, you can put both lists on one page. Don't, however, mix the two together into a grab-bag list.

List charts, tables, and illustrations in the order they appear in the report. They are numbered consecutively, including those that appear in the appendix. Captions, if needed to help explain the tables, usually appear under the table titles in the text but are normally omitted in the list.

Since it follows the contents page, the list of tables is numbered consecutively in lower-case roman numbers—in this case, v.

Synopsis

A synopsis is a condensation of the entire report giving more information than an abstract and weighted more toward results and conclusions than a straight summary (see section 19, "How to Write a Summary"). A synopsis is used in long reports to give the reader a brief overview of the contents. Most writers weave synopsis material into the letter of transmittal by featuring the major points leading to their recommendation. In such a case, of course, the synopsis is not included as a separate unit. Even though compact, a synopsis should be specific, citing all essential information. Since a condensation must of necessity reduce volume, word choice is crucial. Take time to cut and prune the synopsis so that you can say as much as possible in the fewest words. Each section of the report does not receive equal time in a synopsis. Emphasize your results, conclusions, and recommendations, and give only enough of the introductory material so that the reader can follow along. He wants to know what he should do. Make sure the synopsis tells him what and why and how you know. Since the synopsis is often widely circulated—usually without the accompanying report—make sure it stands up logically and coherently on its own.

If you are writing a report on a controversial topic or for a reader who you judge must be convinced, then you will have chosen not to reveal your conclusion until the end of the report. You hope that by then your logical presentation of facts will have led your reader to the inevitable conclusion. In this case you make certain your synopsis contains essential supporting detail.

If used, the synopsis is labeled *Synopsis,* sometimes *Summary, Abstract,* or *Highlights,* at the top center of the page. Number consecutively in lower-case roman numbers at the bottom center of the page.

Do your best to keep the synopsis on one page. Be guided by the length of your report, but consider a ratio of twenty to one rather than ten to one if the section gets too long. Try single-spacing if you need room. A synopsis that is too long defeats your reason for having it. One that is too short or too vague doesn't help the reader.

Introduction

The introduction is the first page of the report proper. As such, arabic number 1 is placed at the bottom center of this page. Subsequent pages (2, 3, 4, . . .) are normally numbered in the upper right-hand corner. Your complete title as it appears on the title page is repeated at the top center of the first page.

The text may be single- or double-spaced, as your needs dictate. However, always avoid a crowded appearance by keeping margins—top, bottom, sides—generous and by leaving white space between sections and headings so they can be seen easily by the page-scanning reader.

Standard introductions typically contain three sections: the *purpose* of the report, the *methods* used, and the *scope* of both the problem and the writer's research.

The *purpose* section shows the reader you understand the task he wanted you to do. The purpose section, or its equivalent, should have one sentence that sums up the problem. Take time to craft the most readable, pointed *statement of the problem* you can. If you find you are unable to come up with one, chances are that you yourself do not understand the point of your report. Needless to say, then, you won't be able to write a clear, logical report. You need more research, a talk with whoever assigned you the task, or both.

The *methods* section tells the reader how you gathered and analyzed the information in the report. In this section you establish the validity of the entire report. Your methods should be explained with enough detail to ensure that the study could be repeated, the experiment reconstructed, the survey duplicated, the same experts consulted again. Thus the major test of your methods section is to ask yourself if you have given the reader all the specifics he would need to duplicate your research and analyze your data.

The *scope* section tells the reader what you intend to cover in the report: how thorough your research, how deeply you have delved into the problem. Now is the time and place to tell him exactly what the report covers and why, and what it does not include and why. Often writers find that they can include an examination of *limitations* within the scope section.

Some additional sections for which you may find use in the introduction include *background, criteria* or *standards*, a separate *limitations* section, a *glossary* or *definition of terms*, and a *plan* or *organization of report*.

Unless very short, the *background* or *history* comes before the purpose section and logically leads the reader through the developments bearing on why the report is being written. When background material is included in the purpose section itself, these two sections are combined. Your guide to whether you need a separate section will be how much explaining you must do to prepare the reader for the *why* of the report. Keep in mind that far too many reports have background sections that are either too long or weren't needed in the first place.

You will want to use a separate *criteria* or *standards* section (see section 23, "How to Write an Evaluation") if you are called upon to

> make a choice
>
> > compare two or more things, like products, services, processes, or forms of organization
> >
> > evaluate one thing according to a set of expectations or standards.

Your standards should be specific, fair, and weighted according to importance. For example, assume you are evaluating a new product because you want to find out if it is cheaper to use than your present choice. You will want to emphasize price as the major criterion. Other standards like convenience, availability, and performance, while important and sometimes crucial, are nonetheless secondary criteria in a cost analysis study.

Usually included within the scope and methods sections, *limitations* may be a separate section if long or complicated. The danger of treating limitations separately is the probable negative effect on the reader. Therefore, be careful that you emphasize the steps you took to overcome difficulties. Use positive phrasing. Don't say, "Mr. Geibel was unavailable the entire month of June so I had to get what information I could from his former assistant, Mr. Robert Armstrong." Instead say, "Even though Mr. Geibel was unavailable throughout June, I was able to get much of the information I needed from his former assistant, Robert Armstrong." Remember a limitations section is not a catchall for excuses. Use it to give legitimate reasons for how and why the report is limited.

You should include a *glossary* (often called *definitions*) so that every anticipated reader can understand your report (see section 14, "How to Define a Term"). However, if your list is long, consider placing it in the appendix. Refer to your glossary the first time you use each item in it in the text.

> (See appendix, p. 21.)
> (See full definition in glossary, p. 4.)

Use a *plan*, or *organization of the report*, section only if your report is long or your organizational approach is unusual. Keep the section brief. Avoid repeating the same words and phrases, such as "Then I will. . . ," "Then I will. . . ."

Body

Present your findings to the reader in the body or middle of the report. Bear in mind that your reader is discovering the facts as he reads. Unlike you, he doesn't have the big picture before he sees the report. Therefore, keep your presentation adapted to your audience. Build your case step by step. Don't try to tell everything all at once and don't leave gaps in your logic. You must, in effect, strike a balance between confusing your reader by presenting too much too fast and boring him with explanations of the obvious. Be certain you present *all* your data. To help you organize them, see section 15, "How to Classify and Analyze." To be sure your report is readable, try testing the "fog" level of your writing. For advice on reducing fog, see section 25, "How to Make Your Writing Complete, Concise, and Easy to Read."

In general try to avoid using abbreviations in running discourse. You may use abbreviations freely in tables, footnotes, bibliographies, lists, compilations of statistics, or anywhere necessary to save space. Some abbreviations are always acceptable in running discourse: for example, *Mr., Ms., Dr., Jr., Sr., Ph.D., B.C.* and *A.D.* when used with a date, and others. For detailed treatment of how and when to use abbreviations, see *Words into Type*, 3d ed. (Englewood Cliffs, N.J.: Prentice-Hall, 1974).

Pages in the body are numbered continuously throughout, normally in the upper right-hand corner. Headings will be more specific here than in the introduction if you used standard headings there. For information on how to cite sources, see section 28, "How to Use Other People's Writing."

Conclusions

The conclusions section has its own heading and is similar to the body in appearance and format. Help the reader by organizing the section logically. Consult section 16, "How to State and Support a Conclusion," to see how to construct this section and where to locate conclusions in the report. They may come before or after the introduction as well as after the body.

Recommendations

If recommendations are asked for in a report, it is a good idea to separate them from the conclusions section. Recommendations are likely to be personal and subjective, and it is wise to keep them apart from conclusions, which should derive strictly from the data. The recommendations section answers the question "What should we do about what we have just learned?"

This section will, like the conclusions section, have its own separate heading and consecutive page numbering. For more information see section 17, "How to Make a Recommendation."

Bibliography

The reader will look in the bibliography to find the sources you used to gather information. The bibliography may list the books, magazines, brochures, and films you consulted or the names of people you interviewed. It will always include those sources that you cite in the text, that yielded significant information, or that you relied on heavily.

Use any logical and consistent format you feel comfortable with. Be guided by traditions in your organization or profession. Order, of course, demands that people's names, books, and articles are not all lumped into one list. Separate them by category and use subheads, such as *People I Interviewed, Articles I Cited,* and so on. The exception is when sources are listed in the bibliography in their "order of appearance," that is, according to the order they are cited in the report. In this case, they are numbered. When the reference appears in the text, only the corresponding number in the bibliography and the page number need be given.

> Davis found that only 11% of first-time offenders who completed the self-rehabilitation program were returned to prison by the courts. (7:23)

The 7 means item number 7 in the bibliography, on page 23 of the book or periodical listed there. If you use this method, you will of course have to explain it to the reader if it is not standard in your office. Tell him how it works in some convenient place in the introduction, or preferably the first time you use it. This form has the advantages of saving space and of not interrupting the flow of your report. If you have a lot of citations in your text, it will also make you a friend of your typist. Whatever method of citation you choose, be sure all possible readers of your report understand how it works.

The bibliography page is titled *Bibliography, Books Cited, Articles Consulted and People Interviewed,* or whatever is appropriate. The page is numbered consecutively in the upper right-hand corner. If in the course of your research you consulted every book on the issue in the Library of Congress, resist the temptation to put them all in the bibliography. List only those that you got direct information from, not those sources you checked but that didn't pan out. Keep the bibliography as brief as your good judgment allows. Remember, as always, that this section too is for the reader's use. If he wants to check on a point or pursue the topic, he can do it with the aid of your bibliography. Don't pad the list with useless items just because you want him to know you spent a lot of time on research. A well-done report is your best guarantee of recognition.

Appendix

Include in the appendix any information the reader will need to check your data, validate your conclusions, or pursue a related point. The appendix is not an attic for all those things you hate to throw away. Its function, like all sections of the report, is primarily to serve the reader. Large chunks of detailed information in the text are awkward to write and dull to read. However, the report must include the complete data somewhere. The appendix is the place. Thus long tables, lists, questionnaires, examples, forms, and analyses that would interrupt or complicate swift reading of the report belong in the appendix. Use abbreviated or summarized versions within the main text (see section 12, "How to Use Charts, Tables, and Lists").

Put in anything you think will help the reader. Many times, compiling a list of related items appearing in various sections of the report is an aid. Should the reader want to refer again to the items, he doesn't have to hunt through page after page to ferret them out. You've done that work for him. You've been helpful, and he'll like that. As you can see, then, the appendix is not a catchall for all the semirelated information you've gathered along the way. Most appendix material does not come ready-made. Like the rest of the report, it has to be organized and reworked into a useful tool for the reader. If the information does not bear directly on the point of the report, then leave it out of the appendix.

Usually appendix material is organized according to the order in which the topics appear in the text. Titling each item is sufficient if you have only a few. If you have a lot of material consider labeling each item by number for handy reference in the text. For example, if you have eight items you can label each of them by both title and number:

Exhibit 1. Names and Addresses of Approved Area Contractors

In either case the reader should never find material in the appendix that he has not been told about in the text. The best time to direct him to appendix information is the first time the topic comes up. Most often a brief parenthetical reference is all you'll need.

Borough engineers evaluated area contractors according to the Contractor Competency Form we drew up for them last year and that was approved by the Borough Council last January. (See Exhibit 7, p. 29, for a copy of the Contractor Competency Form.)

Avoid the temptation to label the entire section *Appendix*. Instead, label each item in it separately. Usually each item is given a fresh page. You may, however, put two closely related short pieces on the same page, but each will have its own title. Be guided by the appearance of the page. If it looks crowded, separate the information. If it seems skimpy, put another list on the page. Center the material attractively. You may put large charts, graphs, and tables sideways in the appendix. Avoid foldouts if at all possible. Often it is preferable to use the back of the preceding page than to resort to a foldout. But, of course, if you must, you must. Be sure to give the reader directions on how the page unfolds. Include "Open here" or "Fold out from center" or "Flip up" or some such directions in a conspicuous place.

The pages of appendix material are numbered consecutively throughout the report in arabic numbers in the upper right-hand corner. If the last page of the text of the report is numbered 21, then the first page of appendix material will be 22.

How to Use Headings

Headings help the reader by labeling sections and parts. Thus if your headings are accurate, easy to read, and neatly presented on the page, they will aid the hurried reader and reward the attentive one. Good headings reveal the organization and logic of a well-reasoned report. They permit quick reference to specific sections and points made in the text. A report with too few or vague headings will look imposing and tedious. Keep your report visually attractive and easy to read by making liberal use of clear headings.

How Specific Should Headings Be?

Make them as descriptive of the material they label as you can. A heading should be inclusive enough to account for all the information contained in the section it titles. It should be exclusive enough to label *only* the material in that section. If, for example, for your own convenience you have called the section that describes your problem, your methods, and your procedures *Introduction*, now is the time to label it properly for the convenience of the reader. Be as specific as you can be: avoid when you can rubber-stamp headings like *Introduction, Body, Recommendations;* they don't really tell the reader anything about your particular report. Of course, it is easy to tell you what not to do and nearly impossible to show you how to do it. You can't be told what to write because your headings should be specifically about your topic. For instance, if your report is about establishing a water purification plant in Atlantic City, then terms like *Water Purification* should appear in your headings. Study the sample table of contents in exhibit K to see how one author did it. Even though it won't help you to copy his method, it might help to see how he tried to make his headings specific. In other words, headings from one report are not interchangeable with those from another. If yours are interchangeable, then they are probably too vague.

How Long Should Headings Be?

Most headings, to be specific enough, are more than a single word or term long. Often they are abbreviated sentences. A good way to get the feel of the function of a heading is to study the headlines of a quality newspaper like the *Wall Street Journal* or *New York Times*. The rule of thumb in determining length is to make the heading long enough to be an inclusive label but short enough to be immediately clear. If you must use abstract rather than concrete words, grapple with difficult concepts, or use any unfamiliar terms, then do your best to limit the heading to one line. Headings that go on to a second line are hard for the reader to use—he can't see at a glance what the section will include. On the other hand, don't be afraid of an occasional two-line heading if you can simplify your terms and explain your topic in concrete, everyday words. The test, as always, is "Will it help the reader to do it this way?" If the answer is yes, then do it. Break any rule if it makes good sense to do so. Just be sure, first, that it does.

How Should Headings Look?

Headings should appear in the text exactly as they appear in the table of contents. If your heading is capitalized and underlined in the table, it should be capitalized and underlined in the body of the report. The wording should never vary. Your headings should look exactly the same in both places. If they do not, the reader will get confused.

How Many Levels Will You Need?

In general, only two levels of headings are shown in the table of contents: the first group of major, or *first-level*, headings that indicate the three or four (possibly five, but no more) primary sections the report falls into, and the *second-level* headings that label the sections within each primary section. Primary headings correspond to items numbered in capital roman numbers (I, II, III) in traditional outline form. Second-level headings correspond to those items in outlines tagged with capital letters: A, B, C. Often, in fact, report writers so number and letter their headings. If you think numbering will help the reader, do it. In your report you probably will want to subdivide your material even more, remembering that, in general, headings make the going easier for the reader. Therefore you will no doubt use *third-level* headings (those that correspond to items labeled in arabic numbers in outlines, i.e., 1, 2) in the test of the report. Third-level headings are not normally included in the table. To do so would crowd the page.

How Should Material Be Divided?

Headings divide the material presented in a report in much the same way that a mother cuts up a pie for her three children. She will take great pains to divide the dessert equally among them. Your headings, too, should be chosen to appear equal—both grammatically and logically. Let's look at an example. Suppose a major section of your report is entitled *Types of Fruit Trees You Should Consider for Long-term Canning Profits* and that you have three subheadings under it:

A. Dwarf Apple
B. Elberta Peach
C. Bartlett Pear

If, in your discussion, you conclude that Bartlett pear trees won't do because pears are really a short-term profit item in your business or because they won't grow properly in your climate, then your division is illogical. You shouldn't have Bartlett pear under a heading that indicates it is a tree that should be considered or that meets your criteria as a long-term profitable canning fruit. Also notice that the first tree, dwarf apple, uses a different *basis of classification* than the others. *Dwarf* is classification according to size, whereas the terms *Bartlett* and *Elberta* are used to classify the trees by *variety*. The author must choose his basis of classification and stick to it.

Consistency of logic and grammatical form in headings makes an easily read, easily understood report. In this example you can also see the advantage of using more specific headings that help explain rather than merely name what is in the section that follows. If this author had used the following more complete headings, very probably he would not have gone astray in the first place:

A. McIntosh Apple Trees Have Low Initial Planting Cost, Heavy and Extended Yield
B. Elberta Peach Trees Traditionally Bear Highly Marketable Fruits
C. Bartlett Pear Trees Yield Easily Canned Fruits for a Loyal and Predictable Canned Fruit Market

By using more detailed headings the author is able to relate the parts to the whole with greater clarity. His subheads now echo his major heading. He not only names the types of trees but by mentioning marketability and cost factors he also shows the reader how each variety can bring those long-term profits mentioned in his major heading.

In addition, remember that you cannot divide something into one piece. Therefore, each time you divide a section or topic of your report, you must use at least two divisions. For example, there can be no A without at least a B, no 1 without a 2, and so on.

Headings should not interfere with readability. Don't use them as a substitute for the text of the report. The reader should go smoothly from one section or division to the next without having to depend on the heading. Thus, one test for readability is mentally to block out section headings to make sure that the report reads smoothly from topic to topic without them.

SECTION 12

How to Use Charts, Tables, and Lists

Because of their imposing layout on the page, charts, tables, and lists command attention—unless, of course, you have overused them. Correctly used, they give the report reader a different way of "seeing" information and, thus, are called "visuals." Use visuals in your report

if your data are complex and using a table or chart will help the reader understand your point

if compiling the data in a table or chart will save the reader time

if a list, chart, or table will conveniently collect information the reader may want to refer to later.

Think of tables, charts, and lists as falling into two groups:

1. Illustrative visuals—used to amplify a point
2. Collective visuals—used to compile data in an orderly way

Using collective visuals in an appendix is a good way to ensure that all your collected data are included in the report. Long tables, charts, and lists will almost always be placed in an appendix. Placing them in the text breaks up the continuity of your writing. Furthermore, the reader may not be willing to hunt through a mass of figures stuck in the middle of the text. On the other hand, you don't want him to have to flip back and forth between your text and the table in the appendix; he may do it once, maybe even twice, but he'll resent the inconvenience and soon give up. The solution is to use bite-sized tables and charts illustrating one point at a time within the text. Such short charts are often made up from larger charts in the appendix but contain restricted information, topically selected and classified. For example, suppose you have in the appendix a collective table comparing three amplifiers according to cost per unit, gain, distortion levels, heat dispersion, and power requirements. Within the text, when you evaluate the units according to cost, select the information on cost from the large chart and use it in short form. Do the same when talking of gain, distortion levels, and so on.

Tables and Charts

Put illustrations near the appropriate text. If you talk about a table or chart make sure the reader can find it by placing it near the discussion of the point it is to illustrate. To be sure that your visual aids help the reader, let each textual chart illustrate only one point. Also, since the reader shouldn't be expected to interpret the data for himself, make sure you point out what the table shows—call attention to trends, relationships, totals, increases, and so on. You can tell much about both the need for the visual and how you've succeeded in integrating it into the report by asking yourself two questions.

First, is the text understandable without the chart? If the answer is "Well, sort of," you've probably done a good job of preparing the reader for the chart to come and, after he has seen it, of explaining what he saw and why it is important or significant. On the other hand, if the text is crystal clear without the chart, question your decision to use it. Maybe it's not necessary. If the text is incomprehensible without the chart, perhaps you are expecting the chart or table to do your work for you. The visual cannot make your point; it can only help you illustrate it. Don't use tables as a substitute for textual analysis; use them to supplement or emphasize it.

Second, can the figure-oriented reader skim the text, study the chart, and get the point? A "yes" answer here says good things about your chart: the title is specific and meaningful; the caption further explains what the chart is there to show; the layout of the chart is visually uncomplicated; the chart illustrates one point; labeling is readable and direct; appearance is uncluttered. A "no" answer tells you the illustration isn't illustrating, that it needs more work. Very likely it is vaguely titled or too complicated.

Be sure to lead the reader into and out of your list, chart, or table by *introducing* it and *concluding* it in the text itself.

Introduce the Visual

A good way to signal your reader that the table is coming up is to tell him. You can say, for example,

Table 12 below shows the interior dimensions of the two cars.

Make sure, of course, that the table is where you say it will be. Also be sure the table you use shows what you say it will show. And even better way to locate the chart for the reader is to do two things in the sentence that directs him to it: show him where it is and tell him the significant point.

From Table 12 below, you can see that the early production Vega had one inch less headroom than the proposed hatchback design.

By subordinating the directions in the introductory phrase, you are able in less obtrusive manner to signal the reader, give directions, and say something significant about your subject. The second example is longer than the first; however, the second is ultimately the more economical method. The information it contains will take two or possibly three sentences if the first example is used.

Conclude the Visual

After the reader has looked at the chart or table, call attention to the significance of it in your text. Readers are interested in totals, trends, increases, decreases, and so forth. Be sure to wrap up your presentation by explaining these points. You can use a variety of methods, depending on the point you want your table to make. For example, if you wish to emphasize a problem in the ascot market, you might write

As you can see, sales of ascots have declined 52 percent this season even though total necktie sales volume increased by a reassuring 14 percent.

But if you want to emphasize the general health of the necktie industry, you might say it like this:

Notice that, even though sales of ascots declined 52 percent, total sales increased 14 percent over last season.

You may also want to suggest reasons for the trends and proposals for encouraging or modifying them at this time.

Don't assume that the illustration will explain itself. What you say in the text to elaborate will depend on your purpose. Suppose you are reporting salary comparisons for four job levels at two locations. The data can be summarized effectively in the table shown as exhibit L. The table displays a certain disparity in salary treatment of employees. If you are not proud of the disparity, you may decide not to comment on the table. You could claim to have done your duty in presenting the data without comment. If, however, you want to be certain the reader gets the full significance, you will say something like "Notice that a

Table 10

Comparison for Average Composite Salaries for
Campus A and Campus B Faculty

Rank	(1) Campus A (No.)	(2) Average Salary	(3) Campus B (No.)	(4) Average Salary	(5) Dollar Difference (Cols. 2 & 4)
Professor	556	$20,507	5	$16,157	+ 4,350
Associate Professor	497	$15,681	7	$14,296	+ 1,385
Assistant Professor	533	$13,008	284	$12,245	+ 763
Instructor	144	$10,461	263	$10,627	− 166
All Ranks	1,730	XXXXXX	622	XXXXXX	XXXXX

EXHIBIT L. SAMPLE TABLE USED TO ILLUSTRATE A POINT

full professor at Campus A earns as much in four years as a professor at Campus B earns in five." Or "Only at the instructor level does the salary at Campus B compare favorably with its counterpart at Campus A." If the gap has been narrowed and you are proud to report the progress, the explanation will be different. The point is that in most cases, if there is an illustration, there should be an explanation, and both should be clear enough to serve the writer's purpose in meeting what he considers to be the needs of his reader. In this matter as in other matters of written communications, let other knowledgeable people check your choices.

Points to Remember

1. Put long, complicated visuals in the appendix.
2. Use bite-size tables and charts in the text.
3. Keep tables and charts as brief as possible.
4. Signal the reader when a table or chart is coming up.
5. Label clearly and specifically.
6. Number tables consecutively throughout the report; also label charts in sequence. Do not, however, mix the two.
7. Use a visual only if it will help the reader understand your point.
8. Don't interrupt the text with a visual; lead the reader into it and out of it.
9. Point out the significance of the table or chart to the reader.
10. Keep the visual as simple as possible.
11. Use white space and labeling to make your visual attractive; make the reader want to look at it.
12. Consider using tables and charts in the appendix as a way to compile and present all your significant data in convenient form.
13. Usually both the title and caption are centered above the chart. But any consistently followed method will do.

Lists

Using collective and illustrative lists can help you present data in a form that the reader can readily understand and remember. Use them whenever you can. Help your reader by collecting information he may want for future reference in a list in the appendix. In the written portions of the report, even as few as two items can be placed in list form to give them emphasis and to break up the formidable look of a page filled with paragraph after paragraph of text. Such short lists usually need no titles or numbers. If the list is the last part of a sentence, remember that it must read as a grammatically integrated unit.

> The Search Committee proposed that the candidate
>   be a college graduate
>   have at least four years experience in COBOL systems
>   and have a proven sales background.

This same series written out would have commas separating the items. Current practice is to omit commas when the series is listed. You may, however, use them if you wish. In most cases, like the example above, you need no punctuation after the sentence fragment leading into the list. Use a colon (or dash in less formal contexts) if the lead-in is a complete sentence. That is, if you could put a period after the lead-in and it would still make sense, then a colon or dash will work properly. Here's an example:

> The class chose to solicit five kinds of pies for the bake sale:
>   cherry
>   blueberry
>   lemon meringue
>   apple
>   coconut custard

Lists are visually dramatic. Since they are highly visual, they draw the reader's attention. Most readers will see and remember information presented in a list better than the same information hidden in paragraph form. Use lists often for emphasis and readability.

How to Make an Introduction

When a reader picks up a report or article, he asks the question "What is this all about?" It is no fun reading if you can't discover the writer's intention and then follow him through an orderly presentation of the material he has selected to fulfill that intention. Make sure that in your introduction you accomplish the following:

1. Identify your intention.
2. Indicate the scope and limitations.
3. Attract the reader.
4. State or clearly imply the profit of the paper (the theme or the one-sentence summary).
5. Identify the areas of discussion to follow.

An introduction may also
    give background information
    show the procedure used to get the data
    make such other comments as may be needed to transmit the information properly.

When you finish the rough draft of a paper, mark the place where the introductory elements end and the discussion begins. After you do that, study the body carefully to make sure you have said what you wanted to say and that you have organized your material in the most effective way. After you are certain that the body of your paper delivers the message you intend, then examine your introduction. Chances are it will need revision. Your preliminary draft was exploratory. You set out to develop a certain topic along vaguely planned lines, but the actual writing probably led to discoveries and a new sense of reality. You must revise the introduction to accommodate what the paper actually says. An introduction promises something. The body delivers something. Be sure the introduction promises only what the body delivers.

The introduction should give the reader all the information he will need to assure him that you understood the problem, that you chose sound methods to investigate it, and that he can rely on your judgment throughout the rest of the report. Opinion won't convince him. Facts and specific detail will. Tell him *what* you did, *when, where,* and *why.* Give names, titles, dates, exact figures. Think of the introduction as a foundation to support the rest of the report. No matter how magnificently you construct the remainder of the report, it won't hold up if the foundation is shaky.

SECTION 14

How to Define a Term

As you go through a rough draft mark any terms that need definition. Deciding what terms to define is not easy. You don't want to insult your reader. On the other hand, you must give him all the help he needs to understand what you say. If the term has a special meaning in your trade or profession, and those outside your profession will read it, define it. If the term does not have wide currency, define it. If the term is widely used, but there is a chance its meaning is vague, define it. Terms like *graduate-level course, high standard of living, technical writing, mental cruelty, religious, racist, seasonally adjusted,* and *unemployed* are frequently used as if everyone knew what they mean. If you are using such a term responsibly and if understanding its meaning is essential to understanding your point, define it.

You can define a term in one sentence simply by adding a synonym in parentheses immediately after its first use:

The window was supported by a corbel (bracket).

or by a variety of direct statements:

We must first agree on what we mean by an alcoholic.

As I use it here the term high standard of living means. . . .

The term *détente* means all things to all people, but for the sake of this discussion. . . .

For a more formal one-sentence definition, place your term into a family and then show how your term differs from other members of that family. If you begin your sentence with

"Blue chip" is the common stock of a company

you have helped the reader by placing the term in a family. Now he knows that a blue chip is not a slice of potato that fell into the indigo. All that remains is to show how blue chip differs from other common stock. Your sentence would logically conclude with

that has an acknowledged reputation for making money in good and bad times.

Often the one-sentence definition is not enough. You may need to extend the definition to a paragraph, a page, or several pages. There are several common techniques for extending a definition.

Comparison and Contrast

Think of all the items you can that are essentially different but have points in common with your subject. Analyze these similarities. This is comparison. Think of all the items or concepts that are essentially the same but have points dissimilar with your subject. Analyze these points of difference. This is contrast. Comparison and contrast are useful techniques of clarification. An especially useful part of contrast is the technique of saying what the term is not, listing the terms that might be confused with it to show their differences, and then winding up with a statement of what it is.

Corpus delecti does not mean the body of a victim of murder. It does not mean proof that there is a corpse. It does not mean charges against a suspect. It means a substantial body of proof that a crime has been committed.

Example, Illustration, Anecdote

Many times the best way to define a term is to tell a little story to show what you mean. Christ did this in the parable of the good Samaritan when someone asked him what he meant by the term neighbor. Here is another example:

The term *assault* means that someone intended bodily harm to another or put another in fear of bodily harm even though none was inflicted. Let me illustrate: Mr. Caine and Mr. Able got into an argument. At one point Mr. Caine picked up a club and chased Mr. Able up an alley. Some men noticed the altercation and took the club away from Mr. Caine. Mr. Caine probably is liable for assault.

Synonyms

It is difficult to find two words that have exactly the same meaning in all contexts. In extending a definition of a term it is useful to show the subtleties of difference in meaning of synonyms. Consider the word *pay*, meaning "the act of one person handing over money to another." Other terms might be more appropriate to your context: *recompense, compensate, remunerate, reimburse, indemnify, reward.*

Word Origin

Some words have interesting histories. Sometimes only knowledge of that history can yield a satisfactory understanding of the term. An example is *gerrymander*, a transitive verb meaning "to rearrange voting districts in such a way as to give advantage to the party in power." The term gained currency after the rearranging of districts in Massachusetts during the governorship of Elbridge Gerry. A map of the resulting district resembled the profile of a salamander. Hence the term *gerrymander*—Elbridge *Gerry*, 1814 American statesman, plus *salamander*, from the shape of an election district formed during Gerry's governorship. One needs to know the origin of the term in order to appreciate the meaning:

> To divide a territorial unit into election districts to give one party an electoral majority in a large number of districts while concentrating the voting strength of the opposition in as few districts as possible—*Webster's New Collegiate Dictionary.*

How to Classify and Analyze

Someone has said that there are two kinds of people in the world—those who divide the world into two kinds of people and those who don't. At any rate, with data coming at us in bundles the need to classify is inescapable. Like things, like concepts must be put in like categories. The hard thing in classifying is to pick the right basis, that is, a basis that enables you to make an interesting investigation. To classify people on the basis of height into the categories short, tall, and in-between is not a profitable exercise. To classify them on the basis of socioeconomic status may be quite useful.

Whenever you are trying to make sense out of a welter of data and can't seem to separate the items into manageable groups, try filling in the blanks in the following sentence:

On the basis of _____, _____ can be divided into _____ groups.

If you can fill in the sentence you can write your paper. Suppose the subject is army officers. Your interest, prior knowledge, and intelligence will lead you to a meaningful basis of classification. Otherwise you will never be able to write because the subject is too varied to manage. So you begin hunting a basis:

On the basis of relationship to troops, army officers can be divided into command and staff.

If you change the basis of the classification, you change the resulting categories:

On the basis of political leanings, the army officer. . . .

On the basis of degree of isolation from mainstream American influences, army officers can be. . . .

The possibilities are endless. And the rules are simple:

1. Get a workable basis.
2. Make sure no individual fits into more than one category.
3. Make sure there is a category for each individual.

SECTION 16

How to State and Support a Conclusion

First, make sure you have a conclusion worth supporting. Then make sure you know whether it is a judgment that can be supported by verifiable facts or a judgment of value or opinion.

Judgments are easier to support if they are not extreme. "Japan must build nuclear weapons" is more difficult to support than "Japan should consider defending itself." In your enthusiasm for your judgment don't beg the question in stating it. The judgment "Japan must give up her notion that she can devote her energy solely to economic growth under the naive assumption that another nation will defend her" includes the question-begging word *naive*. That the assumption is naive must be proved and the assertion must not be offered as evidence in the judgment.

To convince a reader that your judgment is valid you rarely have as much ammunition as you would like, so you must make the best use of what you have. The best form of proof is verifiable fact. Make sure you have all the facts that are applicable to the problem. Also effective is the opinion of an expert. Use it when you can, along with interpretation of facts and the various forms of logical reasoning. Expository forms of definition, illustrating, and analogy, and the rhetorical forms of emphasis, concreteness, conciliation, and refutation, all contribute to the defense of your conclusion.

First there is the introduction, where you tell your reader what you are going to do in the body. Next comes the body, in which you do what the introduction promised you would. Then comes the conclusion, in which you clearly state the profit of the paper. The conclusion answers the question "What does it all mean?" Used this way, *conclusion* means "suitable ending." But in a business report we often need more than a suitable ending. We often need to identify the inferences that can be drawn from the data examined (they can be one or several). A dictionary will tell us that a conclusion is the last part of a chain of reasoning. It is a judgment, decision, or opinion derived from examining a body of information. The conclusion section of a report may contain a summary of the analysis, but it will not introduce new material for analysis. Conclusions should be briefly stated, usually numbered if there are several. They must always be clearly justified by the facts analyzed in the body.

Conclusions are the logical result of the evidence you presented in the body of the report. In most cases readers want to know quickly what you've discovered or decided, so conclusions are often placed out of normal order. They may come before or after the introduction. Of course, location of the conclusions section will determine how you present your data in the body. If you present conclusions first and data later, then you must justify your results with the supporting data. When conclusions follow the body, you must build, like a relentless detective, a case that shows your conclusions to be inevitable. Whichever method you use, beware of overstating your case, lest the reader be put off by your seeming bias. Report writers usually don't intend to write a biased report, although sometimes one will result when the writer hasn't done a complete job of researching. But usually a biased report, or a report that appears biased, is born out of a desire to write a "good" report. Remember that researched data rarely point as clearly as a one-way–street sign. Often some conclusions will support your recommendations while others will not. Do not, however, gloss over conclusions that are puzzling, unpleasant, incomplete, or that don't seem to fit into your scheme. That's writer bias. Report all the conclusions the evidence dictates. If you do, your report will be honest, fair, and, most of all, useful to the reader. He won't be able to act profitably on conclusions that sound good but are wrong or misleading.

When using "conclusions first" order, you will have to explain the why of each result more thoroughly, since the reader has not yet seen the supporting data. Whichever order you use, be as specific as possible when stating results. Give major supporting points and cite significant evidence.

Following are some methods you might want to consider in organizing a conclusions section:

1. Presenting most important results first, less significant later.
2. Organizing results according to the order each subject was reported on in the body.
3. Following the format you may have used in the introduction to explain what the report was undertaken to discover.
4. Reporting positive results first, negative next. Or vice versa.

Choose a method that suits your subject and that will seem reasonable and logical to the reader. Don't abandon organization in the conclusions section; you need it more than ever to present logical, reasonable-sounding results.

SECTION 17

How to Make a Recommendation

Recommendations should be feasible, within the budget of the enterprise, and acceptable to the sense of propriety, morality, and appropriateness of those affected, especially those responsible for any change. Don't try to avoid responsibility for making a recommendation. Don't hedge or try to cover all your bets. If no action at all is safe or clearly indicated, then recommend that nothing be done. If further study is needed, the boss wants to know what you think he should do. Tell him. He may look at the recommendations first. Then when he understands what you want him to do, he will surely examine the data that led to your conclusions. He will look at and think about the details, the enumerations, the logical structures you use to support your argument. He will look for evidence to judge your judgments. He will wonder whether you are responsible, whether you have considered all the hazards, whether your recommendations are excessively motivated by self-interest.

In making recommendations you put yourself on the line. You show what you are worth. Here is where you announce your view of reality. You'd better be right. Show him that you are by mentioning the reasons for your decision, drawn from the conclusions of the report. Say things like "Because ascot sales have slumped so badly in the last two years, I recommend we discontinue the line." Always let the reader know *why* you are suggesting a course of action. Don't force him to flip to another section of the report in order to understand what's going on in the one he's reading. Be helpful in the recommendations section. Suggest other sources of information, alternate courses of action, people he might want to talk to, or how to implement the actions you say he should take. Most important, avoid sounding either indecisive or curt. Don't command; it is better to suggest and recommend.

SECTION 18

How to Edit

Once you have completed the rough draft of your report, you must craft it into the finished product. Here are some guidelines to consider in this reworking.

What You Say

First make sure you haven't left anything out. Then begin the chore of reorganizing and rewriting. Put paragraphs into sensible units that follow one another logically. Make decisions on whether or not information should go in the appendix or be reworked into the text. Get out scissors and Scotch magic transparent tape. (Part of its magic is that you can write on it.) If you think a paragraph might do better elsewhere, try it there. Shuffle and reshuffle. Then read through for continuity. Once you're satisfied you have it, you are ready to make the report readable.

How You Say It

Now begins the editing. You know what you *want* to say; you must find the words to say it. Working on one section at a time, go through the draft literally word by word and ask yourself if that particular word is

necessary
correct
sensible
clear
logical.

Then work on each sentence, using the same tests you applied to the words. Do the same for each paragraph. Be merciless. Throw the deathless witticism out if it isn't needed. Don't fall in love with a line that doesn't work as well as a less clever version. Train yourself to value words that do the job best, not those that you think display you as clever or bright.

As you can readily see, some sections will need many rewritings before you get them into final shape. Some may need no reworking at all. Although it's bothersome, it will pay off in saved time later if you try to keep your current draft as clean and orderly as possible.

You now should have a fairly readable draft, cleared of most debris. You have rewritten the original with the reader in mind; you have made your words as direct and pointed as you could. Now read through the complete report again for continuity. Have others read it, too, and ask them to make suggestions. Finally check grammar, spelling, and appearance, and consult the following list.

Points to Remember

1. Make it readable.
2. Embody in the report a single controlling idea. You should be able to state that idea in a sentence.
3. State a specific aim, some desired result. What do you hope the reader will do after he reads the report? Follow that aim unswervingly throughout the report.
4. Keep tone consistent—generally serious, objective, responsible.

5. Organize. Parts must be treated in the right sequence. A whole must emerge from the parts.
6. Develop your points; that is, craft paragraphs in which elements of the controlling idea are expressed, demonstrated, and validated.
7. Support general statements. Use details, enumerations, examples, evidence, appropriate logical structures.
8. Be consistent in person, tense, voice, and number.
9. Use words that convey precise meaning, not approximate meaning.
10. Use accepted standards of grammar, punctuation, and format.
11. Choose a title that labels the contents. It should reveal or clearly suggest the specific idea of the paper.
12. Be neat and correct in all aspects of manuscript mechanics.
13. Use headings and subheadings to lead the reader through the thought.
14. Keep the report as brief as clarity and completeness permit.
15. After it is typed, proofread the final paper and have errors corrected or pages retyped before submitting.

SECTION 19

How to Write a Summary

A summary is a reduction of a piece of writing to its essential message. The purpose of a summary is to save a reader's time. The reader will get the gist of the original, but he will not have to go through some of the supporting detail, the elaborations, the logical structures that may be necessary to comprehend fully the complexity of the original piece.

The ability to make good summaries is an extremely useful craft. Since many companies ask that each report contain a summary, or an even more brief abstract, sometimes both, you will need to know how to prepare one. In addition to summarizing your own writing, knowing how to reduce lengthy pieces of writing will help you research the work of others as you prepare material for your own report or collect information for the work or use of others. Because those in business need information quickly and often, the person who can shorten volumes of written material into the useful form of a summary is valuable to his company. Here's how it is done:

1. Read the piece carefully and often enough to understand it.
2. Find the thesis—the point the piece is written to make.
3. Mark the parts or the aspects into which the material breaks. What does each contribute to the whole?
4. Extract from each paragraph—or section, depending on the length of the piece—its general statement in one sentence.
5. State the thesis and support it with the essence of each paragraph or section.

This will give you a bare-bones summary almost as spare as an outline. Add additional supporting detail depending on how long you want the summary to be. If a summary is much less than 20 percent of the original it will lose a lot of informative value. If it runs over 50 percent of the original it will not save enough of the reader's time.

An abstract is a brief summary, usually under two hundred words for the average report. The abstract is often seen by others who will not read the report and is frequently detached from the report and circulated or filed separately. Thus, it must stand on its own as a coherent unit apart from the report. Since length is so restricted, the abstract is limited essentially to identifying the project, mentioning anything unusual done, and reporting significant results and recommendations. Study the following examples to see how a summary and abstract are distilled from a longer passage.

ORIGINAL PASSAGE

A Failure to Communicate

The commission's major concern with the news media is not in riot reporting as such, but in the failure to report adequately on race relations and ghetto problems and to bring more Negroes into journalism. Concern about this was expressed by a number of participants in our Poughkeepsie conference. Disorders are only one aspect of the dilemmas and difficulties of race relations in America. In defining, explaining, and reporting this broader, more complex, and ultimately far more fundamental subject, the communications media, ironically, have failed to communicate.

They have not communicated to the majority of their audience—which is white—a sense of the degradation, misery, and hopelessness of living in the ghetto. They have not communicated to whites a feeling for the difficulties and frustrations of being a Negro in the United States. They have not shown understanding or appreciation of—and thus have not communicated—a sense of Negro culture, thought, or history.

Equally important, most newspaper articles and most television programming ignore the fact that an appreciable part of their audience is black. The world that television and newspapers offer to their black audience is almost totally white, in both appearance and attitude. As we have said, our evidence shows that the so-called "white press" is at best mistrusted and at worst held in contempt by many black Americans. Far too often, the press acts and talks about Negroes as if Negroes do not read the newspapers or watch television, give birth, marry, die, and go to PTA meetings. Some newspapers and stations are beginning to make efforts to fill this void, but they have still a long way to go.

The absence of Negro faces and activities from the media has an effect on white audiences as well as black. If what the white American reads in the newspapers or sees on television conditions his expectation of what is ordinary and normal in the larger society, he will neither understand nor accept the black American. By failing to portray the Negro as a matter of routine and in the context of the total society, the news media have, we believe, contributed to the black-white schism in this country.

When the white press does refer to Negroes and Negro problems it frequently does so as if Negroes were not a part of the audience. This is perhaps understandable in a system where whites edit and, to a large extent, write news. But such attitudes, in an area as sensitive and inflammatory as this, feed Negro alienation and intensify white prejudices.

We suggest that a top editor or news director monitor his news production for a period of several weeks, taking note of how certain stories and language will affect black readers or viewers. A Negro staff member could do this easily. Then the staff should be informed about the problems involved.

The problems of race relations coverage go beyond incidents of white bias. Many editors and news directors, plagued by shortages of staff and lack of reliable contacts and sources of information in the city, have failed to recognize the significance of the urban story and to develop resources to cover it adequately.

We believe that most news organizations do not have direct access to diversified news sources in the ghetto. Seldom do they have a total sense of what is going on there. Some of the blame rests on Negro leaders who do not trust the media and will not deal candidly with representatives of the white press. But the real failure rests with the news organizations themselves. They—like other elements of the white community—have ignored the ghettos for decades. Now they seek instant acceptance and cooperation.

The development of good contacts, reliable information, and understanding requires more effort and time than an occasional visit by a team of reporters permanently assigned to this beat. They must be adequately trained and supported to dig out and tell the story of a major social upheaval—among the most complicated, portentous, and explosive our society has known. We believe, also, that the Negro press—manned largely by people who live and work in the ghetto—could be a particularly useful source of information and guidance about activities in the black community. Reporters and editors from Negro newspapers and radio stations should be included in any conference between media and police-city representatives, and we suggest that large news organizations would do well to establish better lines of communication to their counterparts in the Negro press.

In short, the news media must find ways of exploring the problems of the Negro and the ghetto more deeply and more meaningfully. To editors who say "we have run thousands of inches on the ghetto which nobody reads" and to television executives who bemoan scores of underwatched documentaries, we say: find more ways of telling this story, for it is a story you, as journalists, must tell—honestly, realistically, and imaginatively. It is the responsibility of the news media to tell the story of race relations in America, and with notable exceptions, the media have not yet turned to the task with the wisdom, sensitivity, and expertise it demands.[1]

A SUMMARY

The commission's major concern with the news media is not in their riot reporting, but rather in their inability to communicate with both white—the majority of the audience—and black alike. While a large segment of the audience is black, newspapers and television are totally white in both appearance and attitude. This creates a distrust of the so-called white press among blacks. This fact prevents the media from acquiring good contacts, reliable information, and an understanding of the black audience. This in turn limits the media from presenting the total story of the urban problem to both segments of the audience. News media must find ways of exploring the problems of the black and the ghetto more deeply and meaningfully. The commission recommends using the black as a staff member, the black press and radio stations as information agencies, thus creating a relationship within the black community that will allow the media to fulfill their responsibility to tell the whole story of race relations in America.

AN ABSTRACT

The news media have failed to understand what goes on in black America, have poorly presented what they believe they understand, and do not know the real audience for what they disseminate. The improvement of the news media's coverage of black America requires trained black reporters assigned to this beat. The black press and radio should be used. This coverage must be combined with other news coverage in a balanced manner. The presentation of this information must show awareness that the audience is both white and black.

1. *Report of the National Advisory Commission on Civil Disorders*, Otto Kerner, Chairman (New York: Bantam Books, 1968), pp. 382–84.

How to Write a Progress Report

When you are commissioned to write a report, you will often be asked to submit a progress report telling how things are coming along. Like any other report, the progress report should be clear, direct, specific, and well organized. It will have a beginning, a middle, and an end. It will make use of headings and lists to facilitate reading. Yet there are differences. The progress report is normally rather short. Often it appears in memo or letter form. Since the reader is interested in what you've done and what still needs to be done, time order is a natural form of organization for this report. Tell what you've done in the past, what you're doing now, and what you plan for the future.

Title the progress report clearly. Your title will reflect not only the topic of your final report but especially your procedures for gathering information. Remember you are titling the progress report, not the final report. If the title of your final report is to be "How to Get a Private Pilot's License in the Cloud County Area," the title of a progress report might be "Status of My Investigation of Private Pilot License Requirements and Local Facilities" or "My Methods and Procedures for Gathering Information on Your Becoming a Licensed Private Pilot in the Cloud County Area."

Begin the report with a one-sentence statement of the problem and authorization. The reader will want to be sure you understand what you're supposed to do. Show him in detail that you do. Use phrases like *you asked me to, you wanted to know.* Explain in detail how you plan to get the information he needs, what procedures you intend to use, and why. If you take care to craft tight sentences you can do this briefly. Give names, dates, titles. If you say, for example, that you plan to consult "pertinent studies in the field" you really haven't said much, and the reader will know you haven't. If you've done actual digging and come up with significant studies, name them. If you constructed a questionnaire, show it to him. Don't leave him guessing whether it will do what you say it will. Let him see that it will. In other words, include pertinent details of your procedures so that your reader can judge for himself if you're on the right track. After you've submitted the final report, it is too late to discover that you were incorrect in saying that your sampling was "random" in the progress report. You'll avoid problems like that if you say in the progress report how you've gone about finding a "random" sample.

The reader wants to be reassured that you are proceeding correctly and methodically. Give him the *facts* to show him that you are. Avoid assertions of opinion; they simply insist that you know what you're doing. Without facts he won't know whether to believe you or not. He'll lose confidence in your final report before you even write it.

If problems or difficulties have cropped up, the progress report is the place to say so. Since you want to leave the reader with a sense that things are moving right along, however, you won't want to dwell unnecessarily on them. State them as positively as possible. Emphasize the steps you've taken to resolve difficulties. Most problems yield to imagination and increased effort. Nonetheless, occasionally you come up against a limitation that threatens the validity of the entire venture. If so, tell him. Recommend that he reconsider the project. Just be sure that you've examined all the alternatives first.

If you are far enough along in your research to have formed some tentative conclusions, tell the reader. He too is eager to discover how it will all come out. While for the sake of brevity you won't report all the data that led you to your tentative conclusions, give the reader enough information so that he knows why you've reached those conclusions.

If things are going smoothly, end the progress report by confirming the due date of the final report. Try to maintain an upbeat tone to let the reader know that everything is on schedule. If you've run into trouble, emphasize your efforts to adjust the original timetable as little as possible. Keep his confidence. Show him you can adjust to setbacks and follow orders. Let him see that he selected the right person for the job. An example of a progress report is shown in exhibit M.

EXHIBIT M. SAMPLE PROGRESS REPORT IN MEMO FORM

Date: April 12, 19--
To: Ms. Erehart
From: Wilber Rite *W.R.*
Subject: <u>My</u> <u>Methods</u> <u>and</u> <u>Procedures</u> <u>for</u> <u>Gathering</u> <u>Information</u> <u>on</u> <u>Your</u>
Becoming <u>a</u> <u>Licensed</u> <u>Private</u> <u>Pilot</u> <u>in</u> <u>the</u> <u>Cloud</u> <u>County</u> <u>Area</u>

STATEMENT OF THE PROBLEM

On March 16, 19--, you asked me to find out everything you will need to know
to become a licensed private pilot. Since you will be in this area for at least
two years, you wanted to know where to go in Cloud County for qualified instruction.

WHAT I NEED TO KNOW

To make an informed recommendation I must find out
        which airports in Cloud County offer student pilot instruction
        where they are located and the distance from your home
        what is the extent of their facilities and student pilot services
        what is the reputation of the operation and the competency of the
            personnel
        how well the student pilot programs prepare you to meet Federal
            Aviation Administration requirements for licensing
        what additional FAA requirements you will need to know about.

HOW I AM GETTING THE INFORMATION

To gather the information I first called each airport in Cloud County to find
out if they offer a learn-to-fly program. If they did, I scheduled an interview
with an instructor and arranged to be shown around the airport.

I wrote to the FAA asking them for any information they could give me on what
steps must be taken to become a private pilot.

Finally, I planned to check with several members of the local flying club,
Wings Way, to see what I could discover about the individual airports,
specifically the maintenance of equipment and teaching ability of instructors.

WHAT I HAVE FOUND OUT SO FAR

        <u>Who</u> <u>Offers</u> <u>Qualified</u> <u>Instruction</u>: Below are the names and addresses
        of four local airports offering complete learn-to-fly packages:

            1. Cloud Air Park, Cloud County Lane, Cloudland (13 miles
               from your home)
            2. Fly by Night Airport, Route 355, Shillington (17 miles)
            3. Park Air Depot, Junction Hill Road, Junction (8 miles)
            4. Belleton Air Park, R.D. 1, Belleton (22 miles)

In telephone interviews with the managers of all four airports, I found that total costs for package deals, including flight training and ground school instruction, range from a low of $1050 at Park Air Depot to $1500 at Cloud. From what I can determine so far, prices seem closely related to airport facilities, the type and number of airplanes used for training, and services offered the student. Thus far I have visited Cloud Air Park to interview Mr. Rickenbacker, flight instructor, and to tour the grounds.

What the FAA Requires: An aspiring pilot must successfully meet requirements set by the FAA to be licensed. To become a student pilot he must pass a medical examination. To become a licensed private pilot, he must pass a written examination and a practical (flying) examination.

The medical examination is given by three local FAA-certified physicians (see attached list for names and addresses). Preparation for the thorough written test is available in the ground school training offered by the local airports. I will include in the final report a booklet I received from the FAA explaining the test and giving sample questions. Requirements to take the practical examination are met by completing any one of the local learn-to-fly programs.

WHAT I WILL DO SOON

Airport Visits: Within the next week I will visit Fly by Night Airport, Park Air Depot, and Belleton Air Park. At each airport, I am scheduled to talk with an instructor and to be shown around.

Flying Club Interviews: After the airport visits, I have appointments with three members of Wings Way at separate times to discuss their judgments of the airports and the personnel. In an earlier telephone conversation with the club president I was impressed with his openness and eagerness to help. I hope that my talks with the three pilots will give me an "inside" look at what is involved in learning to fly in general and at what these specific airports have to offer.

FAA Material: For the final report I intend to distill much of the thorough information I received from the FAA into a checklist and to explain each examination as it applies to you. For example, I will call one of the local medical examiners to discuss with him what the examination covers and what it costs.

As planned I will have the full report with a recommendation of which local airport can best serve you by May 16, 19--.

Part Three

HOW TO USE
THE TOOLS OF
THE WRITING CRAFT

SECTION 21

How to Dictate

Everybody knows that dictating is more efficient than writing long-hand or typing rough drafts. Everybody *knows* it, but some people still don't *believe* it. They don't believe it because they tried dictating once or twice, and became confused and a little embarrassed. (After all, dictating is in some respects a public performance. Other people in the office hear you fumbling for words and may get an idea that your mind isn't quite the well-oiled machine you'd like them to think it is.) So it's back to the old yellow tablet. It may take a lot longer, but it's comforting to be able to see each word as it comes and to consign your mistakes to the oblivion of your own wastebasket.

Nevertheless, it's well worth while to keep on trying to dictate. If you do, you will soon get good at it, and time spent on routine writing will be cut drastically. Writing is not that much fun. If you can do a better job in fifteen minutes on something that usually takes you an hour, you're better off all around. And savings like this are possible with dictation.

It may help you to realize that you already dictate, no matter how you write. If you scratch out your work on a tablet, your mind is dictating words to your fingers: "Fingers, write out a letter to Mr. John Schmedlap, 101 Braindrain Drive, Dismal Seepage, Alabama. Dear Mr. Schmedlap: The carborundum cherry pitter you expressed interest in is temporarily out of stock," and so forth. The fingers will do what you tell them, but they take a long time; they won't work unless you spell out every word. Since they slow you down, they make you wonder if you are telling them the right thing. You keep judging and second-guessing, and the pile of crumpled paper keeps growing.

It is better to bypass the fingers. Dictate directly to a machine that can record everything you say without slowing you down. Practice will give you confidence and speed. If you make $25,000 a year, every hour is worth $12.81. One hour saved every day for a year is worth a total of $3,126. The people who manufacture and sell dictating equip-

113

ment will be happy to give you detailed instructions in its use. A checklist of essentials is given here to get you started: [1]

1. Identify yourself—name, department, phone number, correspondence symbol, or any other means used by your company. (This applies only when you are dictating into a machine. . . . Your secretary already knows you!)
2. State what you are dictating—letter, memo, report, rough draft or finished product, double-spaced or single, margin size.
3. Identify the priority—when dictating more than one item, give them in order. If your company has a word-processing center, notify the center of high-priority items before dictating. (Otherwise, how will the typist know that your third letter should have been typed first . . . ?)
4. Indicate what paper should be used—company letterhead? If more than one, which? Interoffice memo? Personal stationery? How many copies? What type (e.g., carbons, office copier, or offset)? Must envelopes be addressed?
5. Describe the distribution and identify each receiver—spell out names and addresses. Use the phonetic alphabet for initials. Spell out numbers that might be confusing (e.g., fifty and fifteen, sixty and sixteen).
6. Load brain before firing mouth—decide objectives first; select your points and arrange them in sequence to meet your objectives; organize ideas into paragraphs; break up long sequences into paragraphs; make notes on scrap paper or in margins of the letter you are answering; indicate approximate length of letter (number of paragraphs) in advance and during dictation; indicate each paragraph with a spoken ". . . period. New paragraph."
7. Spell out any words that might give trouble:
   (a) homonyms—*cite, sight, site . . . council, counsel . . . they're, there, their . . . incidence, incidents*
   (b) uncommon—*holocaust, impugn, enigma, renege, surfeit, ensconced*
   (c) foreign—*tête-à-tête, coup, gestalt, viscount, risqué, kaput*

1. The rest of this section has been adapted from "How to Dictate Effectively," a course produced by Dictaphone Corporation, and is used with its permission.

(d) technical—*phenol, emulsified, tensile, viscous, ductile, catalytic, electrolytic, pneumatic*

(e) words that might be misunderstood—*fiscal, physical . . . erratic, erotic . . . formally, formerly . . . abeyance, obeyance . . . era, error . . . monetary, monitory*

8. Dictate all punctuation—commas and parentheses, colons and semicolons, quotes, apostrophes, hyphens, dashes, question marks, and periods.
9. Spell out all mechanical instructions—paragraphs to be indented beyond the regular margins, quotes to be given special margin treatment, columns of figures, entries to be numbered and aligned, titles to be underlined, space to be left for illustrations.
10. Maintain voice control:
    (a) relaxed, normal conversational tone
    (b) not too fast (especially on material that's familiar)
    (c) avoid mumbling, smoking, chewing (pencil or gum), fumbling with instrument
    (d) use appropriate inflections and pauses
    (e) signal instructions to typist (e.g., change tone, give beeps, use his or her name).

The Anatomy of a Dictator

Have you ever stopped to think of the many steps involved when Mr. A dictates a letter to Mr. B? Let's examine them in sequence and in slow motion. This process begins with an initiating event. That is, some stimulus or thought prompts Mr. A to write Mr. B. (Perhaps it is a letter from Mr. B or maybe Mr. B is a prospective customer whose name has been given to Mr. A.)

Mr. A must now clarify his objectives: What does he want Mr. B to do after receiving the letter? That is, what is the desired outcome, or action to be taken? Given this objective, he then organizes his thoughts and decides what he wants to say to Mr. B. That is, he begins to form a mental outline of the message. Perhaps he makes a few notes on a scratch pad (or in the margin of Mr. B's letter, if he's responding to one). If he needs to refer to any facts or figures from the files, source book, or catalogs, he gathers these materials so that he has all references at hand. He then makes arrangements for someone to intercept any phone calls or personal visits so that he can then block out all interruptions to his train of thought. Finally, he *sits down with secretary or dictating machine* and begins to dictate.

His initial directions relate to the mechanical instructions that the typist must know: how many copies, when needed, first draft or finished product, what letterhead, in No. 10 envelope or with mailing label for other enclosures, and so on. He then dictates the receiver's name and address, spelling all words that might give difficulty. In dictating the body of the letter, Mr. A keeps two receivers in mind. First there is Mr. B, whose reaction to the letter is important. So he is careful to select words that will bring his message to life for Mr. B. But Mr. A must also consider another receiver: the person who will type his letter. Thus, he is careful to give instructions on spelling, punctuation, and format wherever there might be confusion or ambiguity.

When he receives the typed letter for signature, Mr. A proofreads it for errors of spelling, typing, punctuation, and so on. He notes corrections lightly in pencil, making his notes in the margin rather than in the body of typed copy (see exhibit N). If text-editing equipment is used, corrections can be made directly in the body, since the corrected letter will be automatically retyped. Thereafter, Mr. A receives the corrected copy and checks the corrections. He then erases the penciled corrections (or makes them on a file copy, where they may remain). Mr. A then checks the address on the envelope or mailing label (and checks to see that any indicated enclosures are present). Finally, he signs the letter and places it in the mail or his out basket.

Corrections to be made in letters, or in any other single-spaced typewritten material, can often be most clearly indicated with proofreaders' marks (see exhibit O). These traditional symbols, widely used by printers and publishers, were devised specifically for use where spacing requires that corrections be indicated in margins.

Law Offices
Henry F. Bruce
10 Nassau Street
Princeton, New Jersey 08540

March 15, 19--

Lewis Gresham, Esq.
Wykoff, ~~Porter~~, and Gresham   *Parker*
Coun(c)lors at Law   *sel*
1600 North Peach Tree Road
Atlanta, Georgia

Dear Lou: *Lew*

    Are you planning to ~~make it seem~~ next week at the   *make the scene*
regional meeting of the Council on criminal justice in
Washington, D.C.?

    The thought occurs to me that we might squeeze in a
little tennis out at Georgetown. I'm bringing my ~~racquet~~ — *racket*
You may want to bring yours (along with some pocket change
to buy my ~~Two Birds~~)   *Tuborg*

    Incidentally, I read your article in the law review on
~~the~~ ~~Marks versus~~ Nationwide ~~case~~. Well done! I'd like to   *Marx v.*
know more, since I have an ~~eminent~~ hearing for a client ~~whose~~   *imminent* / *who's*
been similarly charged. I'm specifically interested in your
~~illusion~~ to the pending ~~statue~~ legislation is forth coming in   *allusion* / *statute*
New Jersey.

    Perhaps you could bring the ~~Mark's~~ brief with you.   *Marx*

Best regards,

HFB/tlr

EXHIBIT N. SAMPLE DICTATED LETTER, PROOFREAD AND MARKED FOR CORRECTION

Similar Sounds: Spell 'em Out

WORDS	MEANING
accept	to receive
except	to exclude
adapt	to suit to
adept	proficient
adopt	to tailor, modify
advice	(noun) counsel
advise	(verb) to give counsel
affect	to influence, to change
effect	(noun) a result; (verb) to bring about
all ready	prepared
already	previously
assent	consent
ascent	rise
cite	to summon, to quote
sight	(noun) a view; (verb) to see
site	a place
coarse	common, rough
course	a direction of progress
commence	to begin
comment	(noun) a remark; (verb) to remark
correspondents	writers
correspondence	letters, other written communication
counsel	(noun) advice; (verb) to advise
council	a group, an assembly
decent	proper, respectable
descent	(noun) act of descending
descend	(verb) to come down
dissent	(noun) disagreement; (verb) to disagree
deposition	testimony
disposition	disposal, temperament
digression	deviation
discretion	judgment, prudence
dissolution	termination, breaking up
disillusion	to free from false impression
enforce	to force, to compel
in force	in power, in effect

WORDS	MEANING
elicit	to draw out
illicit	illegal, improper
enclose	to place within
inclose	in legal use, preferred in speaking of land
exceed	to surpass
accede	to agree
formally	ceremoniously
formerly	in times past
forth	away, forward
fourth	the number: 4
farther	in space
further	in thought, in space
later	comparative form of *late*
latter	second of two mentioned
loose	unattached, free
lose	to suffer loss
precede	to go before
proceed	to begin, to continue
release	(noun) liberation; (verb) to free
relief	aid, comfort
relieve	to ease, to remove burden
they're	(contraction of *they are*)
their	(possessive pronoun)
there	(adverb showing location)

The Phonetic Alphabet

A—Alpha	J—Juliet	S—Sierra
B—Bravo	K—Kilo	T—Tango
C—Charlie	L—Lima	U—Uniform
D—Delta	M—Mike	V—Victor
E—Echo	N—November	W—Whiskey
F—Foxtrot	O—Oscar	X—X-Ray
G—Golf	P—Page	Y—Yankee
H—Hotel	Q—Quebec	Z—Zulu
I—India	R—Romeo	

ℐ or ℓ	Delete		ℓ	The pr∅of
∧	Left out, insert		∧	T∧e proof
#	Insert space		#	The#proof
⌣	Less space		⌣	The⌣proof
◯	Close up; no space		◯	The pro◯of
tr	Transpose		tr	A (proof good)
lc	Lower case		lc	The P/roof
=	Capitals		=	the proof
stet	Let it stand		stet	The proof
spell out	Spell out		spell out	King (Geo)
no ¶	No paragraph; run-in		no ¶	marked.⌐Three men
⌐	Raise		⌐	The proof
⌐	Lower		⌐	The proof
⌐	Move left		⌐	The proof
⌐	Move right		⌐	The proof
∨ ∨ ∨	Insert apostrophe or quotation marks		∨	The boys proof, Marked it proof
[/]	Insert brackets		[/]	The Jones boy
(/)	Insert parentheses		(/)	The proof 1

How to Limit a Topic

Many investigations fail because the writer tries to deal with a topic too broad to handle in one paper. Remember, if you don't have a properly limited topic, you don't have a topic. Here are some suggestions for reducing scope:

1. *Reduction by number:* Instead of an examination of absenteeism in all departments, limit the study to absenteeism in one, say, the typing pool.
2. *Reduction by kind:* Instead of dealing with all kinds of personnel problems in one study, limit the study to one kind, e.g., absenteeism.
3. *Reduction by aspect or part:* Absenteeism may be caused by physical illness, mental or emotional upsets, alcoholism, job dissatisfaction, and other interrelated reasons. A study limited to one of these would be more manageable than one directed to all.
4. *Reduction by time:* Causes of employee absenteeism on Monday mornings.
5. *Reduction by some human element:* A case history of the absenteeism of Marjorie Clinkenbeard.
6. *Reduction by place:* Absenteeism among unclassified employees of the loading dock of the Johnson Plant.
7. *Limit by motive or cause:* Why people choose to miss work.

Broad topics immobilize a writer. Limited ones generate specific detail. By running through the techniques of limiting a topic you can find out what you want to say about a subject.

How to Write an Evaluation

Sometimes you struggle with a piece of writing without realizing that your main purpose is to evaluate something. How good is a chair, a car, a film, a book, a personnel policy, an office procedure, a fellow worker?

When you praise or condemn something, you shouldn't do it just in personal terms—"I like it," "He's a very good man," "It has served us well in the past"—though personal preferences have a place. What you need most is a set of objective standards against which you can compare the items under consideration:

What is an item supposed to do?
What characteristics would an ideal thing of this kind have?

Your standards should be fair. Consider the price range, the geographical and historical context. It's not fair to condemn a lantern because it is harder to light than an electric lamp, or a Volkswagen because it is not so roomy and comfortable as a Cadillac, or a Cadillac because it is more costly to repair than a Volkswagen. Keep the standards as objective as possible. Don't say, "It should be comfortable." Say, "The seats should have four inches of foam rubber padding." Don't say, "It should be fast." Say, "It should accelerate from 0 to 60 mph in under 9 seconds."

After you have the standards for the ideal, then set down the characteristics of the thing you are evaluating. Compare the two. Then judge how well your subject compares to the ideal.

This procedure is helpful even in writing a letter of recommendation for an employer or friend. Ask yourself these questions: What are the ideal qualities a person holding this job should have? What are the characteristics of the person I must write about? How well do they compare to those of the ideal?

122

Notice in the following example how the use of specific standards helps the reader judge the value of the criticism.

AN EVALUATION OF FOCUS BOY SUNGLASSES

As you requested, I have examined the pair of Focus Boy sunglasses you sent me. You are quite right in assuming the importance of good sunglasses. They reduce eyestrain and improve vision. More important, when worn during the glare of the day they greatly assist the eye in its adjustment to darkness. A person whose unprotected eye must fight harsh glare during the day may suffer up to 50 percent loss of night vision. While the loss is not permanent, it may last as long as a week.

Good sunglasses should possess certain qualities. I'll tell you what these are, and then I'll tell you how your glasses compare with the ideal.

Lenses should be of prescription quality and precision ground. They must filter out ultraviolet and infrared rays. Plastic and inferior glass will not do this. The lens must allow no more than 30 percent of the light to pass, and preferably not much more than 20 percent. It should be impact resistant. Gray and sage green are the best colors for lenses.

Frames, which must not be the clip-on type, should have templets not more than one-half inch wide. Hinges should be strong, screws accessible and capable of being tightened, and there should be a metal core running throughout.

The lenses of the sunglasses you sent me are carefully contoured, and they pass quite satisfactorily the flourescent light test. You might check this yourself to see what I mean: Hold the glasses under a flourescent lamp in such a way that the lamp is reflected into your eye. Then tilt the glasses slowly. You will see no distortion, no bumps or squiggles. You can do another simple test. Put on your glasses and look into a mirror in a normally lighted room. If you can see your eyes clearly, too much light is passing through the lenses. I estimate that your lenses allow no more than 25 percent to pass, which is well within the desired range. Then, too, they are the right shade of gray and they are impact resistant. So, you see, your lenses are of high quality.

Your frames are less satisfactory. The one-inch templets are too wide, interfering with side vision. There is no metal reinforcing core, and one of the screws already has stripped threads.

In summary, let me say that your lenses are well suited to your need. If you let me place them in frames of equal quality you will have sunglasses to give you comfort and protection for many years.

How to Get Data from Books

Most people in management positions do not go to work on Monday morning hoping the boss will greet them at the door with a request for a report on something. The words "Get me a report on that" are, in truth, usually heard with a sinking feeling akin to pain. The source of the pain, when it happens to you, is the terrible knowledge that you know precious little about the subject assigned. Worse than that, you don't especially *want* to know much about it. If you had much interest in it, you would probably already know a lot about the subject. Then, the boss would call you into conference to pick your brain, and the ensuing conversation would be almost fun. But you have little knowledge and less interest and there you are, face to face with the boss. And it's Monday morning. What do you do?

First, don't show a moment's annoyance. Your lack of interest is not the fault of the subject, or of the boss either. Subjects are not interesting or uninteresting: they are just there. John Ciardi said it and you should memorize it: "Anything looked at significantly *is* significant." Thus, anything looked at with interest becomes interesting.

Apply this antidote to lack of interest in a report topic. At first you may have to fake it. Smile and look excited as you respond to your boss: "Why yes, Mr. Curtis, I've often wondered why our employees seem to prefer eating lunch at Mac's Bar and Grill rather than at the company cafeteria. I'll be glad to do the study and get you the report by the 26th." Leave quickly, before your smile gets too rigid.

But soon you must generate *real* enthusiasm for the subject. Begin by asking yourself some questions: What makes a company cafeteria popular—or at least acceptable? Who has a good one? Aside from talking with employees and the supervisor of the cafeteria and the friendly short-order chef and mixologist at Mac's, you will want to read existing articles and reports on cafeteria management. You can be certain there will be some—in the company library, in the local city library, in university libraries.

Overcome any sense of awe you may have about books, card files, indexes, libraries, and librarians. There is nothing difficult about library research. If you can open a drawer, if you know the alphabet, if you are not afraid to ask questions of librarians, you can usually uncover one good clue, and that clue will lead you to others and to more and more data. Hunt, look, ask. Something will turn up.

When you find a book, article, or pamphlet that you can use, fill out a card so that later you will know all the details of publication in case you need to cite the source. You can buy printed cards like the one shown in exhibit P or you can use a 3 by 5 index card. So long as you put the needed information on it, either type of card will work. Put the call number down because you might want to look at the source again later. Give each item a reference number. Any number will work so long as each is different. *Imprint* means who published it, when and where.

EXHIBIT P. SAMPLE BIBLIOGRAPHY CARD AND SAMPLE NOTE CARD

CALL NO	TOPIC:	REF NO
AUTHOR		
TITLE		
IMPRINT		
COMMENT		

BIBLIOGRAPHY CARD

TOPIC:	REF NO:
NOTE:	
LOCATION:	

NOTE CARD

When you take notes from the source, do it any way that works, but remember that you will need to shuffle notes. If you have not become used to some other way, use cards like the one shown in exhibit P or stick to index cards. On each note card write the topic the note covers, put in the number you gave to the source—the other card, remember—and make your note. (See section 28, "How to Use Other People's Writing.") Then record the location; usually the page number is all you will need. When you have gathered all your data you will be ready to sort your notes and write the rough draft.

Now that you are armed and ready to deal with source material once you find it, how do you start the search?

Whatever the subject, some of the information you want probably exists. The investigation you want to begin has probably already been done to meet a similar problem somewhere else. A report similar to the one you must write may exist. Thus, the report writer in management must know some of the bibliographical sources available to him so that he can pick up a clue and follow a trail. The lists [1] offered here are very good places to start.

Business Operating Guides and Handbooks

Handbooks that treat specific phases of business operation often contain practical information. Only a few examples of the many types available are listed below.

Apollo Handbook of Practical Public Relations. 1970. Alexander B. Adams. Apollo Editions, 201 Park Avenue South, New York, N.Y. 10003. This is a guide for the nonspecialist who wants to get his organization's message to the public. Includes suggestions for preparing news releases, making speeches, and other aspects of communications.

CCH Federal Tax Guide. (Control edition includes weekly reports.) Commerce Clearing House, Inc., 4025 West Peterson Avenue, Chicago, Ill. 60646. Has authentic information with tax control methods for practical and competent guidance to ensure effective tax management.

Credit Management Handbook. 2d ed., 1965. Credit Research Foundation. Richard D. Irwin Inc., 1818 Ridge Road, Homewood, Ill. 60430. Explains how to organize and operate a credit department, to make credit decisions on

---

1. Adapted from *Basic Library Reference Sources,* Small Business Bibliography No. 18, prepared by Bernice T. Clarke and Terry E. Nelson (Washington, D.C.: Government Printing Office, 1975).

orders and accounts, to collect overdue accounts, and to use credit reporting and rating agencies.

Foreign Commerce Handbook (3813). 17th ed., 1975. Chamber of Commerce of the United States, 1615 H Street, NW, Washington, D.C. 20006. A guide to sources of information and services for exporters and importers. Gives types of service of U.S. government, intergovernmental, and private organizations in foreign trade and related matters. Information sources under sixty major subjects, includes a bibliography of further references.

Marketing Handbook. 2d ed., 1965. A. W. Frey, editor. Ronald Press Company, 79 Madison Avenue, New York, N.Y. 10016. A comprehensive reference book for people concerned with marketing goods and services.

Office Management Handbook. Harry L. Wylie, editor. Ronald Press Company, 79 Madison Avenue, New York, N.Y. 10016. Gives standard principles and practices for running an efficient office, large or small.

Production Handbook. 3d ed., 1972. Gordon B. Carson, editor. Ronald Press Company, 79 Madison Avenue, New York, N.Y. 10016. Gives information about plant layout and location, production planning and control, quality control, and manufacturing processes.

Purchasing Handbook. 1973. George W. Aljian, editor. McGraw-Hill Book Company, Inc., 1221 Avenue of the Americas, New York, N.Y. 10020. Gives thorough treatment of purchasing department organization, management, and operating procedures.

Tax Guide for Small Business. Annual. Internal Revenue Service, U.S. Department of the Treasury. Available at district offices of Internal Revenue Service. Designed to assist businessmen in the preparation of their federal tax returns. Discusses tax problems incident to conducting a trade, business, profession, or acquiring or selling a business.

Directories

Business firms often need information concerning products, potential buyers, or trade associations. Directories of various types are available. The most obvious are telephone books and their classified sections. Many libraries keep some out-of-town telephone directories for business reference. Further listings are available at most libraries.

Guide to American Directories. 9th ed., 1975. B. Klein Publications, Inc., 11 Third Street, Rye, N.Y. 10580. Gives information on directories classified by industry, by profession, and by function. Useful for identifying specific directories to aid in locating new markets or sources of supply.

Federal Government. Rev. ed. U.S. Library of Congress, Washington, D.C., Government Printing Office. A directory of information resources in the

United States with a supplement of government-sponsored information analysis centers.

Encyclopedia of Governmental Advisory Organizations. Quarterly. Gale Research Company, Book Tower, Detroit, Mich. 48226. A reference guide to federal agency, interagency, and government-related boards, committees, councils, conferences, and other similar units serving in an advisory, consultative, or investigative capacity.

Associations

Directory of National Unions and Employee Associations. Biennial. U.S. Department of Labor. Government Printing Office. Gives facts about the structure and membership of national and international labor unions.

Encyclopedia of Associations, vol. 1, *National Organizations of the United States.* Biennial. Gale Research Company, Book Tower, Detroit, Mich. 48226. Lists trade, business, professional, labor, scientific, educational, fraternal, and social organizations of the United States; includes historical data.

National Trade and Professional Associations of the United States and Canada and Labor Unions. Annual. Columbia Books Publisher, 934 Fifteenth Street, NW, Washington, D.C. 20005. Lists the name, telephone number, address, chief executive officer, size of staff and membership, and year formed of more than 4,000 national business and professional associations.

Financial

Dun & Bradstreet Reference Book. Six times a year. Contains the names and ratings of nearly three million businesses of all types located throughout the United States and Canada. (Dun & Bradstreet also publish other specialized reference books and directories, for example, *Apparel Trades Book and Metalworking Marketing Directory.*)

Moody's Banks and Finance. Annual, with twice-weekly supplements. Moody's Investor Service, 99 Church Street, New York, N.Y. 10007. Indexes more than 9,700 American banks and financial institutions, listing their officers, directors, and other top-level personnel.

Rand McNally International Bankers' Directory. Semiannual. Rand McNally & Company, Box 7600, Chicago, Ill. 60680. Lists over 37,000 banks and branches, giving their officials, and statement figures. It also includes the American Banking Association's check routing numbers for all U.S. banks, and a digest of U.S. banking laws.

Government

The following references include directories of municipal, state, and federal agencies, their personnel and functions.

Municipal Year Book. Annual. International City Management Association, 1140 Connecticut Avenue, NW., Washington, D.C. 20036.

Book of the States. Biennial. Council of State Governments, Iron Works Pike, Lexington, Ky. 40500.

State Bluebooks and Reference Publications. Council of State Governments, Iron Works Pike, Lexington, Ky. 40500. A selected bibliography of bluebooks, reports, directories and other reference publications produced by various departments of each state.

Congressional Directory. Annual. Joint Committee on Printing. Government Printing Office. Biographical data on members of Congress, membership and staff of congressional committees; directory of the executive and judiciary, diplomatic corps; and other useful information on federal and state agencies.

Directory of Post Offices. Annual. U.S. Postal Service. Government Printing Office. List of post offices by state, alphabetical list, and post office addresses for army and air force installations.

Sources of State Information and State Industrial Directories. Triennial. Chamber of Commerce of the United States, 1615 H Street, NW., Washington, D.C. 20006. Contains names and addresses of private and public agencies that furnish information about their states. Also listed, under each state, are industrial directories and directories of manufacturers published by state and private organizations. Some regional directories are included.

United States Government Manual. National Archives and Records Service. Government Printing Office. The official organization handbook of the federal government containing descriptive information on the agencies in the legislative, judicial, and executive branches. Abolished or transferred agencies are listed in an appendix.

Individuals

The following lists only the most general works. *Who's Who* directories are also available for specific occupations and locations.

Current Biography. Monthly. H. W. Wilson Company, 950 University Avenue, New York, N.Y. 10452. Extensive biographical data on prominent contemporary personalities.

Standard & Poor's Register of Corporations, Directors and Executives. Annual. 3 vols. Standard & Poor's Corporation, 345 Hudson Street, New York, N.Y. 10014.

Who's Who in America. Biennial. Marquis–Who's Who, Inc., 200 East Ohio Street, Chicago, Ill. 60611.

Who's Who of American Women. Biennial. Marquis–Who's Who, Inc., 200 East Ohio Street, Chicago, Ill. 60611.

World's Who's Who in Finance and Industry. Marquis–Who's Who, Inc., 200 East

Ohio Street, Chicago, Ill. 60611. Biographical information of men and women prominent in finance, industry, and trade.

Manufacturers

In addition to the directories listed, there are available many state manufacturers' and industrial directories. These are too numerous to list here. Ask your librarian if such a directory is published for the state in which you are interested.

Conover Mast Purchasing Directory. Annual. 3 vols. Conover Mast Purchasing Directory, 270 St. Paul Street, Denver, Colo. 80206. Alphabetical listing of manufacturers showing product lines, code for number of employees, addresses, and telephone numbers. Classified section lists products with names and addresses of manufacturers. Special chemical and mechanical sections, and trademark and trade name identification.

MacRae's Blue Book. Annual. 5 vols. MacRae's Blue Book Company, 100 Shore Drive, Hinsdale, Ill. 60521. Lists sources of industrial equipment, products, and materials; alphabetically arranged by product headings. Separate alphabetical listing of company names and trade names.

Thomas' Register of American Manufacturers. Annual. 11 vols. Thomas Publishing Company, One Penn Plaza, New York, N.Y. 10001. Purchasing guide listing names of manufacturers, producers, and similar sources of supply in all lines.

World Trade

International Yellow Pages. The Reuben H. Donnelley Corporation, 235 East 45 Street, New York, N.Y. 10017. Lists business and professional firms and individuals from 150 countries throughout the world under headings that are descriptive of the products and services they have to offer in worldwide trade.

Economic and Marketing Information

The nation's economy and, in turn, its marketing trends are changing constantly. Businessmen can keep abreast by using the current books, booklets, and periodicals as issued by commercial firms and government agencies. Much of the basic statistical information in the economic and marketing areas is collected by the federal government. Commercial organizations use these data and supplement them with surveys of their own. Listed below are some basic reference publica-

tions that present statistical and marketing information; many are issued on a continuing basis.

Books and Booklets

*Bibliography of Publications of University Bureaus of Business and Economic Re-
search.* Association for University Business and Economic Research, University of Colorado, Boulder, Colo.

Business Statistics. Biennial. U.S. Department of Commerce. Government
Printing Office. Supplementary and historical data for the economic statistics published in the *Survey of Current Business.*

County and City Data Books. Bureau of the Census, U.S. Department of Commerce. Government Printing Office. Presents statistical information on
business, manufacturers, governments, agriculture, population, housing,
vital statistics, bank deposits, and other subjects. Issued every several
years.

Data Sources for Business and Market Analysis. Nathalie D. Frank. Scarecrow
Press, Inc., 52 Liberty Street, Box 656, Metuchen, N.J. 08840. Provides market research information, its origins and retrieval. Gives basic sources and
specific references for the study of business trends.

Dictionary of Business and Economics. 1977. Christine Ammer and Dean S.
Ammer. The Free Press, 866 Third Avenue, New York, N.Y. 10022. Defines
more than 3,000 terms in current use, including terms in business law, accounting, banking and finance, econometrics, price and income theory, and
economic theory. Also has entries on important business organizations, interest groups, and publications.

Directory of Business and Financial Services. 1974. Mary M. Grant and Norma
Cote, editors. Special Libraries Association, 235 Park Avenue South, New
York, N.Y. 10003. An annotated listing of several hundred business, eco-
nomic, and financial services.

Editor & Publisher Market Guide. Annual. Editor & Publisher Company, 850
Third Avenue, New York, N.Y. 10022. Tabulates current estimates of population, households, retail sales for nine major sales classifications, income
for states, counties, metropolitan areas, and 1,500 daily newspaper markets.
For each area, gives information on transportation and utilities, local newspapers, climate, and employment. Includes state maps.

Rand McNally Commercial Atlas and Marketing Guide. Annual. (Leased on an
annual basis.) Rand McNally & Company, Box 7600, Chicago, Ill. 60680. An
extensive U.S. atlas presenting marketing data in the form of maps and area
statistics.

SM's Survey of Buying Power. 1974. Sales Management. 633 Third Avenue,
New York, N.Y. 10017. Gives population, income, and retail sales estimates
for state, county, and metropolitan areas (as defined by *Sales Management
Magazine*).

Sources of Business Information. 1964. E.T. Coman, editor. University of California Press, Berkeley, Calif. 94729. Guide to general sources with coverage for specific fields of business and industry.

The Statesman's Year Book. Annual. S.H. Steinberg and John Paxton, editors. St. Martin's Press, Inc., 175 Fifth Avenue, New York, N.Y. 10010. This book is a storehouse of information on the United Nations, all countries of the world, and each of the fifty states of the United States.

Statistical Abstract of the United States. Bureau of the Census, U.S. Department of Commerce. Government Printing Office. The standard summary of national statistics, includes information on the labor force, population, business enterprises, and national income.

Statistical Services of the United States Government. Annual. Bureau of the Budget. Government Printing Office. Serves as a basic reference document on U.S. government statistical programs.

Statistics Sources. 4th ed. Paul Wasserman, editor. Gale Research Company, Book Tower, Detroit, Mich. 48226. Arranged in dictionary style, it cites periodicals, yearbooks, directories, and other compilations issued by state, federal, and foreign agencies, associations, companies, universities, and other organizations.

U.S. Government Periodicals

The following are some of the basic federal government periodicals that contain business and general economic reports and are widely used by businessmen for keeping abreast of developments in their specific areas of interest.

Construction Review. Monthly. U.S. Department of Commerce. Government Printing Office. Brings together virtually all the government's current statistics pertaining to construction, plus some nongovernment statistical information.

Current Industrial Reports. Bureau of the Census, U.S. Department of Commerce. Lists of titles and prices available from the Bureau of the Census, Washington, D.C. 20233. These reports give information at the factory level for different industries on inventory, production, shipments, and other business activities.

Current Business Reports. Bureau of Census, U.S. Department of Commerce. Includes a series of four reports: *Weekly Retail Sales Report; Advance Monthly Retail Sales Report; Monthly Retail Trade;* and *Retail Annual Report.* Government Printing Office. Estimated sales of retail stores by kinds of business and some data for regions and metropolitan areas.

Economic Indicators. Monthly. Prepared for the Joint Economic Committee by the Council of Economic Advisers. Government Printing Office. Presents tables and charts dealing with prices, employment and wages, production and business activity, purchasing power, credit, and federal finance.

Federal Reserve Bulletin. Monthly. Board of Governors of the Federal Reserve System, Washington, D.C. 20551. Has monthly tables of financial and business statistics. Interest rates, money supply, consumer credit, and industrial production are some of the subjects included. Special articles cover the state of economy, financial institutions, statistical methodology.

Monthly Labor Review. U.S. Department of Labor. Government Printing Office. The medium through which the Labor Department publishes its regular monthly reports on such subjects as trends of employment and payrolls, hourly and weekly earnings, working hours, collective agreements, industrial accidents and disputes, as well as special features covering such topics as automation and profit sharing.

Monthly Wholesale Trade Reports: Sales and Inventories. Bureau of the Census, U.S. Department of Commerce. Government Printing Office. Reports trends in sales and inventories. Also gives some geographic data.

Survey of Current Business. Monthly. U.S. Department of Commerce. Government Printing Office. Includes statistics and articles on significant economic developments. Presents statistics on national income, business population, manufacturers sales, inventories, and orders. Carries special articles on personal income, foreign trade, and other aspects of the economy.

General Reference Sources

Almanacs

For short factual information, consult the yearly almanacs. These are available for reference at any library or may be purchased from local bookstores. Like the two listed below, most are published in both hardbound and paperback editions.

Information Please Almanac. Simon & Schuster, 630 Fifth Avenue, New York, N.Y. 10020.

World Almanac. Doubleday & Company, Inc. 501 Franklin Avenue, Garden City, New York 11530.

Encyclopedias

Among the encyclopedias available are *Collier's Encyclopedia*, *Encyclopedia Americana*, *Encyclopaedia Britannica*, and the *World Book Encyclopedia*.

Specialized Encyclopedias

The more specialized encyclopedias include *Van Nostrand's Scientific Encyclopedia, McGraw-Hill Encyclopedia of Science and Technology, Encyclopedia of Banking and Finance, Encyclopedia of Chemistry, Encyclopedic Dictionary of Business Finance,* and *Accountant's Encyclopedia.*

Information Services

When the information being sought is too recent to be in almanacs and encyclopedias, consult the following, which are available at most reference libraries.

Facts on File: A Weekly Digest of World Events. Facts on File, Inc., 119 West 57 Street, New York, N.Y. 10019. This useful and time-saving weekly index digests significant news of the day from a number of metropolitan dailies. The indexes are cumulated quarterly, then annually.

Public Affairs Information Service Bulletin. Weekly. Public Affairs Information Service, Inc., 11 West Fortieth Street, New York, N.Y. 10018. Cumulated five times a year, bound annual volume. A selective subject list of the latest books, government publications, reports, and periodical articles, relating to economic conditions, public administration, and international relations. An especially useful feature is the extensive listing of many types of directory.

Where to Find Publications

Commercial Publications

Most libraries have reference sources for identifying books, periodicals, and periodical articles. For additional listings of books, consult the following.

Cumulative Book Index. Monthly. H.W. Wilson Company, 950 University Avenue, Bronx, New York 10452. A subject-title-author index to books in the English language. Gives price, publisher, number of pages, and date of publication for each book.

Books in Print. Annual. 4 vols. R.R. Bowker Company, 1180 Avenue of the Americas, New York, N.Y. 10036. An author and title index to books currently available from major publishers.

Forthcoming Books. Bimonthly. R.R. Bowker Company, 1180 Avenue of the Americas, New York, N.Y. 10036. This service provides a regular updating of *Books in Print.*

Subject Guide to Books in Print. 2 vols. Alphabetized. R.R. Bowker Company, 1180 Avenue of the Americas, New York, N.Y. 10036. Useful reference for identifying books currently available on a specific topic.

Newspapers and periodicals can be identified through use of the following index listings.

Ayer Directory of Newspapers and Periodicals. Annual. Ayer Press, 210 West Washington Square, Philadelphia, Pa. 19106. A geographical listing of magazines and newspapers printed in the United States and its possessions. Listings are also given for Canada, Bermuda, Panama, and the Philippines. An alphabetical index and a classified section increase its usefulness.

Business Publication Rates and Data. Monthly. Standard Rate and Data Service, Inc., 5201 Old Orchard Road, Skokie, Ill. 60077. Contains a descriptive listing of business magazines and latest advertising rates. Indexed by name of magazine and business fields covered.

National Directory of Newsletters and Reporting Services. Gale Research Company, Book Tower, Detroit, Mich. 48226. Provides basic facts concerning the type of periodical publication not covered in the bibliographic tools concerned with the conventional types of periodicals, such as national, international, and selected foreign newsletters, association bulletins, information and financial services.

Standard Periodical Directory. Biennial. Oxbridge Publishing Company, Inc., 1345 Avenue of the Americas, New York, N.Y. 10019. Gives comprehensive coverage to periodicals in the United States and Canada. Lists over 70,000 entries, including magazines, journals, newsletters, house organs, government publications, advisory services, directories, transactions and proceedings of professional societies, yearbooks, and major city dailies (weekly and small daily newspapers are excluded).

Ulrich's International Periodicals Directory. Biennial. 2 vols. Merle Rohinsky, editor. R.R. Bowker Company, 1180 Avenue of the Americas, New York, N.Y. 10036. Volume 1 covers scientific, technical, and medical periodicals; volume 2 covers arts, humanities, business, and social sciences. Classified by subject.

Articles in business and professional magazines provide current information. Specific subject indexes to periodical articles, such as those listed below, are available at libraries for reference.

Applied Sciences and Technology Index. Monthly. H.W. Wilson Company, 950 University Ave., Bronx, N.Y. 10452. Subject index covering periodicals in the fields of engineering, applied science, and industry.

Business Periodicals Index. Monthly. H.W. Wilson Company, 950 University Ave., Bronx, N.Y. 10452. Subject index covering periodicals in the fields of business, finance, labor relations, insurance, advertising, office management, marketing, and related subjects.

Readers' Guide to Periodical Literature. Semimonthly, except monthly in July and August. H.W. Wilson Company, 950 University Ave., Bronx, N.Y. 10452. A general index to periodicals such as the *New York Times Magazine.*

Federal Government Publications

Most U.S. government publications report research and activities of various federal agencies. Some are free from the issuing agency; others cost a nominal fee. Most federal agencies issue, periodically or intermittently, lists of their current publications. (If not available at local libraries, these lists are free from the issuing agency. Check with the nearest field office of the government agency. For local office addresses, look for the agency under "U.S. Government" in your telephone directory.) Since most of these publications are relatively inexpensive and are usually among the most recent and authoritative writings in a particular field, they can be very helpful to the public.

By law, the established system of government depository libraries makes federal publications available for public reference. Libraries designated within this system can elect to receive from the Superintendent of Documents, Government Printing Office, those classes of federal publication appropriate to their type of library reference service.

The Superintendent of Documents also issues a number of price lists (single copy, free) on selected federal (for-sale) publications related to specific subjects, such as "Finance" (PL 28), "Commerce" (PL 62), and "Census" (PL 70). For a complete list of the price lists available, request *How to Keep in Touch with U.S. Government Publications,* free from the Government Printing Office. Various price lists can also be consulted in depositor libraries.

Almost every public library regularly receives listings of materials currently available from federal agencies, and most librarians keep them handy for ready reference. The most comprehensive is the *Monthly Catalog of United States Government Publications,* issued by the Superintendent of Documents, Government Printing Office. It lists by agency both printed and processed publications issued each month, including congressional hearings, documents, and reports.

The Small Business Administration also issues two listings of currently available management assistance publications: "Free Management Assistance Publications" (SBA 115A) and "For-Sale Booklets" (SBA 115B). Both lists are free from the nearest SBA field office (consult your local telephone directory) or from the Small Business Administration, Washington, D.C. 20416.

State Publications

The *Monthly Checklist of State Publications* includes all state documents received by the Library of Congress, listed by state and issuing agency. Most reference libraries will have a recent issue, as well as current and historical material of local civic interest, including newspapers, magazines, and books.

SECTION 25

How to Make Your Writing Complete, Concise, and Easy to Read

Complete means nothing has been left out. *Concise* means no more words than necessary have been used to convey the meaning with an appropriate tone. A piece of writing can be complete and short. It can be concise and long. Completeness can best be checked by careful reading and reworking of rough drafts. Conciseness is a little more difficult. (That old rule "Avoid all unnecessary words" is useless. If you knew they were unnecessary you wouldn't have used them in the first place.) What you must do is edit—cross out, tighten up. Nobody can write concise prose on the first draft all the time. Ask yourself "Must I say it at all?" If you must, your next question is "What is the clearest, shortest, most direct way of saying it consistent with good manners?"

Recommendation: Dictate your first draft fairly quickly, without undue judgment. Ask for a triple-spaced rough draft. Then edit mercilessly. (For a glossary of handy phrases to use and wordy expressions to avoid, see section 31, "How to Control Troublesome Expressions.")

To make sure that your writing is complete and readable, consider the following suggestions:

1. Lead your reader through your thought. Repeat key words in the title, introduction, and topic sentences.
2. Check to make sure that you have made your points in a logical order and that you have supplied all logical transitions.
3. Keep your sentences short. There's nothing wrong with having a long one every now and then, but work to keep the average under 20 words.
4. Don't let subordinate clauses run to more than one-third of the sentence. Keep subordinate clauses under ten words. Try not to put one between a subject and a verb.
5. Use parentheses, brackets, underlining, dashes, and question marks freely, wherever it makes sense to use them. They tend to make reading easier. Use exclamation marks sparingly. Overuse lessens their effect.
6. List items by number or letter when appropriate. Lists are easy to read. Maps, charts, and tables may help too.
7. Use familiar, concrete words whenever you can.
8. Use the word you need, but try to find synonyms of one or two syllables for the long ones. One- and two-syllable words should account for at least 80 percent of your words.
9. Use contractions when an informal tone is appropriate.
10. Watch out for redundancy.
11. Try to avoid noun clusters (called noun-adjuncts) like *childhood sex education* and *the new curriculum committee.* The reader must pause to figure out whether you mean education about childhood sex or sex education for children. He must hesitate because he doesn't know if you mean a committee to discuss the new curriculum or a new committee.
12. Try to get a verb into the act in every ten words. Don't let nouns do the work a verb should do. "There will be a meeting of the safety committee in room 103" is not so direct and readable as "The safety committee will meet in room 103."
13. Prefer verbs in the active voice, especially when writing about people. Make them the subjects of verbs whenever you can. It is easier to read "Dr. Vincent Greene developed a new heart valve" than it is to read "A new heart valve was developed by Dr. Vincent Greene."
14. Consider the size, style, and placement of type on a page. Use white space generously. Margins, line spacing, and indentations all contribute to reading ease. A cramped format can make it difficult for a reader to get your message.

15. Ask a knowledgeable reader to examine your edited draft. Pick someone who won't mind telling you the awful truth. False or uninformed approval will do you no good. If the criticisms make sense to you, revise your draft to accommodate them. Don't allow another to distort your own view of the truth, but keep in mind that management writing must please a reader, get a job done, smooth a relationship, clarify an issue, and not necessarily bolster your own ego.

Don't try to follow all these suggestions at once. They are not inflexible rules, merely guidelines to help you in drafting and editing. Ignore any of them any time you want to get a special effect.

To check your writing for readability, you can use the following test for foggy prose:

1. Mark out samples of 100 words each (stop counting with the sentence that ends nearest to the 100-word total).
2. Divide the number of words in all the samples by the number of sentences. This will give you the average sentence length.
3. Count the number of words of three or more syllables in each 100 words. Don't count proper nouns. Don't count words which are combinations of short, easy words—like *money-changer*—or verb forms that get their third syllable by adding *es* or *ed*, as in *adapted*.
4. Add the average sentence length and the number of hard words per hundred.
5. Multiply the sum by .4. The resulting number corresponds to grade-level reading ability. Nine means read easily by a ninth-grade student. Much business communication can be shared at the ninth-grade level. A score of 13 or more is probably too troublesome to be read willingly by most people.[1]

Another widely used readability scale [2] involves a similar view of what produces easy reading: Keep sentences short; keep the number of syllables per hundred words as low as possible consistent with the need to use the exact word; use personal pronouns liberally when possible; and use words that have masculine or feminine gender.

1. For a detailed discussion, see Robert Gunning, *The Technique of Clear Writing*, rev. ed. (New York: McGraw-Hill Book Company, 1968), pp. 36–39.
2. See Rudolf Flesch, *The Art of Readable Writing* (New York: Collier Books, 1962), pp. 224–25.

SECTION 26

How to Prepare Minutes of Meetings

Much time is spent and, it is alleged, some work accomplished by groups of people sitting at huge mahogany tables discussing alternative courses for the good of the enterprise. Although management people gripe about committee work, they generally enjoy the give and take of purposeful argument. They are especially pleased when they feel they have persuaded a group to accept their view of reality.

You can be certain, however, that one person at the meeting is not having fun. That person is the one who was appointed to make a record of what the committee discussed and decided—to prepare the "minutes of the meeting." It's not a job anybody ever asked for. It often falls to the person least in a position to refuse. When it falls to you, do your sighing and grumbling as inconspicuously as possible and then get on with it.

Embrace the job with enthusiasm. You might as well, since you can't get out of it. It is really an excellent proving ground. You will be the only person at the meeting who knows what is going on because you will be listening and taking notes, not rehearsing the speech you will make as soon as you can get the attention of the chair. You will learn a great deal about that modern management mystery, "organizational dynamics"—the art of persuading groups. And you will learn to write. Your minutes will be "published," that is, circulated, certainly to the members of the committee and possibly beyond.

Here is a list of what you must do in these minutes:

1. Name the group.
2. State the time, place, and date of the meeting.
3. List the subjects discussed in such a way that the reader can find a single item without reading the whole report. Make effective use of headings and white space. (For help with headings see section 11, "How to Use Headings.")

140

4. Summarize the various discussions. (See section 19, "How to Write a Summary.") Boil the summary out of your voluminous notes. You will need all your skill as a reporter. Report the facts, not the emotional tone of the meeting, and never inject your subjective view of the proceedings.

> NOT: At this point, Mr. Tibbett announced sarcastically that the company symbol, the brass monkey we have all come to cherish, has outlived its usefulness and that, since it costs the company ten thousand dollars a year just to have the thing carried indoors every night the temperature falls below freezing, the committee should recommend that the symbol be changed to something more supportive of the image we wish to project or at least to something less costly to maintain—like the stately hemlock. Mr. Harrison slammed his notebook on the table and, like a six-year-old kid, threatened to resign if there were any more irresponsible talk like that. After much wrangling, the committee decided to keep the brass monkey.

> BUT: Mr. Tibbett suggested that the committee consider the hemlock as a possible replacement for the present company symbol. Mr. Harrison demurred. The committee discussed the proposal at length and voted not to recommend a change at this time.

5. Record decisions made, and if responsibility is fixed for any procedure, be sure to name names and due dates.
6. If the group is small, list the names of those in attendance. Consider, too, listing the names of those absent so that a month or two later it will be easy to see who did and did not participate in a discussion or decision.
7. Identify the chairman.
8. Identify yourself as the person preparing the minutes.
9. Check your rough draft carefully. If possible, show it to one or two people who were in the meeting.

Then have the final version typed, reproduced, and distributed, frequently with a cover memo giving agenda, time, and place of the next meeting. Such a distribution of minutes is shown in exhibit Q.

EXHIBIT Q. SAMPLE COVER MEMO AND ATTACHED MINUTES

Swanee Tire Exchange

To: All Store Managers   May 12, 1977

From: Edgar Tredd, Secretary, Store Managers Committee

Subject: Announcements for the next store managers meeting

Next Meeting

May 26, 1977, at 8:00 P.M. in the Conference Room at the Wayside
Inn, Middletown. Please note: The starting time for this meeting
is 8:00 P.M., one half hour later than usual.

Tentative Agenda

1. Approval of the minutes of the April 23 meeting (attached).

2. Reports: Simplified Inventory Procedures--Mr. Parelli

        Expanded Store Hours--Ms. Todd

        Plans for the Company Picnic--Mr. Kennard

3. Guest demonstration: Mr. McNab from Levee Advertising Co.
   will show the new series of store window signs the Exchange
   ordered for the July 4 Tire Sale.

4. Chairman Radcliff's remarks

Swanee Tire Exchange
Store Managers Meeting

Minutes of the Store Managers Meeting, April 23, 1977

Chairman Radcliffe called the meeting to order at 7:30 P.M. in the
Conference Room at the Wayside Inn, Middletown.

The minutes of the March 19 regular meeting and the March 26 special
meeting were accepted.

Mr. Radcliffe presented Ms. Vulcan, new manager of the Mayfield
store.

Reports

1. A report prepared by the Blimp Rubber Company on the long-range
effects of the current labor unrest was read and discussed. One strong
recommendation was for each store manager to increase his stock of
cappable casings.

2. Mr. Kennard reported briefly on the outcome of the trial methods
used in the Harmon Mall store to keep customers out of the service
area. A customer waiting area with magazines, a coffee table, and
chairs in the corridor works if customers are politely asked to wait
there. Signs are ignored.

Tips for improving sales and service

Mr. Radcliffe asked each store manager to share with the group any
tips for improving sales and service. A summary of these suggestions
follows:

1. Managers should spend half of their time outside the store promoting sales, calling on commercial accounts, talking tires to everyone
they meet. Managers should be at least as aggressive as insurance
salesmen.

2. While tires are being changed, have a service man check the battery.
A recent check at the Martindale store showed one battery out of six to
be close to failure. Since beginning the practice, the Martindale store
shows a 23 percent increase in accessory product sales.

3. Instruct store personnel to push trade-ins. Many customers, especially those with comfortable incomes, are not interested in getting the last mile out of a tire. They prefer the feeling of security that comes with a set of new tires. Sound tires traded in this way can be resold to less affluent customers who should be encouraged to replace their hazardous bald tires. Make all drivers tire-safety conscious.

Chairman's announcements

1. Customers who neglect to take the 2 percent discount should be reminded to do so. Store managers must continue to carry the credit on all accounts and cannot divert the discounts to any other purpose.

2. Mr. Radcliffe asked all store managers to check the employment records of all tire men they hire, making sure all months for the past five years are accounted for. He cited the case of an employee who was discharged by the Mayfield store for stealing tools and hired at the Reese Corner store the same afternoon.

Assignments

Ms. Vulcan agreed to find a guest speaker for the August Awards Dinner. She will work with Mr. Dayton who is in charge of the Awards Dinner program. Both will report to the committee at the June meeting.

The meeting was adjourned at 9:05 P.M.

The following persons attended: G. Babbitt, C. Balchon, T. Dayton, L. Kennard, P. Lorge, T. Radcliffe, A. Todd, E. Tredd, S. Vulcan

The following managers did not attend: D. Parelli, H. Whitewall

Respectfully submitted,

Edgar Tredd

Edgar Tredd, Secretary

How to Write a Memorandum

A memorandum, usually called a memo, is a standardized form used for sending written communications within an organization from one department to another or from one person to another. It is usually brief, usually informal. The subject is usually limited.

The memorandum is used for routine communications much as the telephone or as conversations in the hallway or across desks, but it is used instead of conversation whenever a record must exist of the matter discussed. Spoken words evaporate, and the person who did not deliver something he promised over coffee can claim the conversation never took place or that it made an entirely different point. The memo fixes responsibility. Also, complexities do not get lost.

Format is simple: there is a line to show who should get the message; a line to show who sends it; a line to show what the message is all about; and a date (see exhibit R). Headings are used if appropriate.

EXHIBIT R. SAMPLE MEMO SHOWING FORMAT

MEMORANDUM

To Wanda Newcomer   *Subject* Memorandum, definition of

From John Veteran J.V.   *Date* July 12, 19--

A memorandum, usually called a memo, is a standardized form used for sending written communications within an organization from one department to another or from one person to another. It is usually brief, usually informal. The subject is usually limited.

Other conventions of effective writing are observed. The memo, just as other forms of business writing, must be clear, concise, correct, and in good taste. No signature is needed, although some executives sign theirs and many initial theirs right after their typed name in the *From* line. In other respects custom varies from company to company or organization to organization, and all newcomers should review the practices of their group.

SECTION 28

How to Use Other People's Writing

You are working on a report or article and come across a passage that would help your argument. You know, of course, that if you copy it word for word without quotation marks and without acknowledgement, you are guilty of stealing, and the owner may be able to collect damages in a lawsuit. What are your options for the proper use of such material?

First, resist the urge to quote at length. Quote when you must, but consider alternatives first. Remember that facts, meanings, thoughts, and ideas cannot be copyrighted. Only the writing expressing them can be. Try to paraphrase the passage; that is, put it into your own words after you have thought the ideas through and thoroughly understood them. Paraphrase the ideas expressed, not the sentence patterns of the original. Organize your version to suit your own understanding of the reality expressed. Then acknowledge the source in a footnote or directly in the text.

> To paraphrase George Orwell, the more careless we become with language, the more language deteriorates and the more slovenly our habits with language become.

If you continue paraphrasing, you will need to remind the reader.

> Orwell also suggests that. . . .

Be careful not to pass off apt expressions in the original as if they were your own. If you like some writer's apt expression, use it and give him credit.

> In the apt term of Bernard Baruch, there is a "maturity of custom" that. . . .
>
> It is what William Vaughan Moody would call a "dull commercial liturgy."
>
> This is an example of a dull commercial liturgy (William Vaughan Moody's term).

In the foregoing examples, the use of an apt term helps make a point. Literary allusions that you use to emphasize or illustrate a point usually require mention of only the author's name, rather than a full citation. Some references are so well known that they have become a part of the language and require no citation:

> Unless the trainee program is completely reformed, eventually we can expect the management level of this company to deteriorate to a Babbitt mentality.

Whether you will need a full citation, giving the author, title, place and date of publication, and page number, depends on your use of the source and your judgment of the familiarity your readers have with it. When paraphrasing authors in your field whose work is famous, a full citation is often unnecessary. However, you should document fully when you think a reader might wish to look up the original—either as a check on your accuracy or for his own use. Always give a full citation when the work or opinion of another, no matter how well known, is central to your point. As you read, note the way other writers attribute thoughts and words to their sources. Follow such good examples in your own writing.

If the idea you want to use is so perfectly expressed that any translation into your own words would lessen its effect, you may want to use it as it is written. Sometimes, using a direct quote lends authority to the point you are making. Be sure you transcribe the passage exactly as it appears in the original; don't quote out of context, and don't distort the intention of the author you are quoting. Show, by quotation marks or indentation and spacing, that you are quoting, cite the source, and you cannot be guilty of intellectual dishonesty.

Usually, you will want to put shorter quotations, those under ten typewritten lines, within quotation marks in the text. You can weave the citation into the text if it is not so long that it disrupts easy reading.

> As Timothy Green points out in *The World of Gold* (New York: Walker and Company, 1968), p. 219, "the world's bankers must lay their plans on the assumption that the volume of newly mined gold will steadily go down."

If the citation is rather long, you may want to use a footnote. Note, however, that footnoting is an unpopular form of citation in business writing. Many readers are distracted by being pulled from the text to a footnote at the bottom of the page or to a list of notes at the end of a report. Others have been put off by the overuse in the past of Latin abbreviations. The difficulty footnotes present in typing makes using them even more troublesome.

A better alternative to footnoting is to put brief, parenthetical citations in the text and to consign all bibliographic details to a reference list appended to the end of your report. In this way, you can keep your text uncluttered while identifying your sources for any reader who wants to track them down. If you are not sure that all who may read your report will understand the system you are using, explain how it works the first time you use it.

Here is how a brief-form citation would look in the text:

> . . . whose time has come: nonetheless, "for boards and administrators to plunge their schools into it without advance preparation carries great potential harm for regular and special students and for teachers as well" (Ryor, p. 5).

In the reference list, the reader would find complete data:

> Ryor, John. "Mainstreaming" (editorial). *Today's Education* 65 (March–April 1976), 5.

Naturally, if you cite more than one author with the same surname or more than one work by the same author, you'll have to supply more information in parenthetical citations. Give the full name if different authors share the same last name. Use the last name with a shortened form of the title to distinguish works by the same author. If you can't be clear and keep this form of citation brief, use another system. You might want to try the one described in section 10, "How to Set Up a Full-Dress Report," under the heading *Bibliography*.

Longer quotations, or those you may wish to give special emphasis, are indented, without quotation marks, and single-spaced. You can weave the citation into the text that leads into the quote, as shown earlier. Better yet, use a brief form of citation in the lead-in or following the quotation. Note that if the author's name is mentioned in the lead-in, you need give only the page number when using the brief form.

The same point is made by Karl Marx (p. 159):

If footnoting, place the number after the quote or after the author's name if it appears in full in the lead-in (see exhibit S). The name of the author is not repeated in the footnote if it is given in full in the text.

Once a source has been fully cited, subsequent footnotes for the same source should be brief, yet clear. Avoid using Latin abbreviations. The following is sufficient for a second reference to Semenow's *Questions and Answers on Real Estate:*

2. Semenow, p. 189.

EXHIBIT S. SAMPLE FOOTNOTE FORMS

. . . the decision to expand the marketing program for

Product CB100:

> Any company that seizes a commanding market share in
> a new field is thus fortified for the roller-coaster ride
> that typically reduces costs by a factor of 10 every five
> or six years.[1]

1. Victor K. McElhany, "Revolution in Silicon Valley," The New York Times, June 20, 1976, Sec. 3, pp. 1, 11.

According to Robert W. Semenow[1]

> a real estate broker is not personally responsible for
> an error or mistake which he honestly makes, unless
> he has been careless, grossly negligent, or has gone
> contrary to his honest convictions and beliefs.

1. Questions and Answers on Real Estate (Englewood Cliffs, N.J.: Prentice-Hall, Inc., 1972), p. 86.

Whatever method of citation you choose, use it consistently throughout the report or article. Remember that, besides crediting others, the point of citing is to enable a reader to locate the quote or reference in the source. Make sure you supply enough information so that he can.

Occasionally, you will have to decide if you need permission to quote. You do not need permission to quote any works in the public domain, that is, works not copyrighted, such as most material in government publications, or works on which the copyright has expired. Much business writing, even when "published"—that is, widely distributed—is not copyrighted. Though you may be under no legal requirement to cite the source, courtesy often demands that you do. Follow the practice of your company and be guided by your own good sense.

If the material is copyrighted, you may still quote it without permission under certain limits. Each publishing house tries to set these limits to suit its own circumstances and to simplify its own operating procedures, and there is not much uniformity among houses. One house may expect authors to ask permission to quote 150 words from an article; another may tolerate many more. Journals using the American Psychological Association *Publication Manual*, 2d ed., permit use of 500 words of text without explicit permission. Some houses (most members of the Association of American University Presses, for example) permit use of up to 1000 words from a single book. Courts of law, however, do not use length to decide questions of fair use. They use percentage of the whole and the context in which the quoted material is used. The main concern seems to be the amount of loss or damage the owner suffers from your use of his material. The University of Chicago Press *Manual of Style*, 12th ed., rev. (Chicago, 1969), p. 93, offers this advice: "If the quoted passage is from a published work in prose and not an entity of any sort within a larger work and if its use does not detract from the value of the original, the author should probably *not* ask permission to use it, regardless of length."

The foregoing quotation is from copyrighted material. It is an insignificant percentage of the original work, not an entity of any sort within a larger work. Its use here enhances (we hope) rather than detracts from the original, so we will follow the owner's advice and not ask permission to use it. In section 19, "How to Write a Summary," we have quoted a much longer passage from the Kerner Report. We have not asked permission to quote it because, as a government report, it is in the public domain. Even if it were under copyright, we think its use in this book as an example of a prose passage suitable for summarizing does not detract from the value of the original, and it is a very small proportion of the total size of the original report. There is an element of risk in any assumption one makes about the fair use of literary property. Let's hope there will be none in the project you are working on—or in the ones we have just cited.

How to Construct Good Sentences

In belles lettres, or writing as art as distinguished from technical and scientific writing, a good sentence is a mystery. You know one when you see one, but you could not draw up a prescription for writing one. Let's examine a few candidates for the good sentence award.

> And I felt like I did when I was a boy and it was time to get up and go out and play all day Saturday. (Jack Kerouac)

This sentence violates a few conventions. Yet, if you wanted to show a middle-aged man suddenly discovering joy again, how could you improve it?

> Draw your chair up close to the edge of the precipice and I'll tell you a story. (F. Scott Fitzgerald)

Here the promise of terror, without using the word, makes the sentence effective.

The artistic writer dealing with joy and terror and other emotions has options not available to the management writer. The management writer does not want echoes and suggestions and reverberations of meaning. He wants only the one meaning he intends. When the novelist says, "In all thy orifices may my sins be forgiven" (John Barth), the mind quivers for five minutes matching orifices to sins and considering the marvel of forgiveness. An attempt to get so much into nine words of management writing would probably be disastrous.

In management writing, any sentence that conveys a thought with economy, precision, and regard for the reader's interest is a good sentence. The advice of this book is to practice simplicity. Although fortunately your choice is not that restricted, it is better to be simple to the point of monotony than to be complex to the point of obscurity.

The sentence is the building block of the report. Only as good sentences work together can good paragraphs take shape. A superior in a religious order when asked by a novice how to become a saint replied, "First, you have to stop sinning." The advice in this section is similar: To write good sentences you must first stop writing bad ones.

But before you read all the bad news about how your sentences can go wrong, here's some good news. Remember those three rules of usage your English teacher drilled into your head long ago? You were taught (1) not to split an infinitive, (2) not to begin a sentence with *and* or *but*, and (3) not to end a sentence with a preposition. Well, you can relax a bit. Violating these precepts does not necessarily result in a faulty sentence.

You should not hesitate to split an infinitive if the sense of the sentence requires that you do. Consider this sentence, for example:

> He hoped to more than double his income in the following year.

It is a good sentence; yet, the infinitive is split, and needs to be. Of course, you shouldn't split an infinitive without carefully noting its effect on the sentence. If the resulting sentence is clumsy or unclear, a split infinitive may be causing the problem. But a sentence that is clear and graceful can easily survive a split infinitive.

Beginning a sentence with *and* or *but* has the same usefulness to a writer than the fragment has. In fact, this use often works well with a fragment.

> Any public official who uses expense accounts so lavishly may find himself in the ranks of the unemployed. And ought to be.

Beginning a sentence with *and* or *but* can be an effective technique so long as you don't use it so often that it loses its dramatic effect for the reader. Naturally, if you overuse the technique, the reader will begin to anticipate it and won't be surprised. Save the technique for those times you want to achieve a special effect.

The controversy over ending a sentence with a preposition is finished. It started because some people thought that anything named *pre-position*, because of its name, always had to be placed before something, that something must always come after it. The unnatural contortions needed to comply with such a rule led to its abandonment. (Riled by a pedantic proofreader who applied this rule, Churchill once reportedly quipped, "This is the sort of impertinence up with which I will not put.")

Following are discussions of ways sentences go wrong. Learn to avoid the errors identified in each example and you will be well on your way to producing sharp, crisp sentences—most of the time. All right, then, some of the time.

Faults in Sentence Unity

A sentence gets into no trouble so long as it expresses one thought.

> John sold 50 shares of Ajax Can.

However, see what happens when simple sentences are used to show relationships:

> John sold 50 shared of Ajax Can. Ajax Can is the world's largest maker of trout flies. The Alpha Company merged with the Beta Company. Alpha Company makes horseshoes. Beta Company makes horseshoe nails. The demand for trout flies has fallen off. The demand for horseshoes has increased. The demand for horseshoe nails has increased. John bought 50 shares of Alpha-Beta.

Somehow, it doesn't all "fit." The pieces of the puzzle are there, but the writer has not put them together for the reader to understand quickly and easily what happened and why. The job of the writer is more complex than simply listing thoughts and letting the reader figure out how they fit together. The writer must show, through the use of sentence structure, how the ideas relate to each other. Selecting the proper structures will highlight important ideas and deemphasize less significant ones. By making relative order out of absolute equality, the writer creates meaning and significance. But selecting the right structure is never easy.

Trouble comes when you try, as you must, to get more into and out of a sentence than you can if you take ideas one sentence at a time. When additional ideas are expressed in the same sentence, the relationship of the ideas to each other must be clear in the construction of the sentence. If two values are equal, they must be phrased in equal structures:

> The Alpha Company has been making horseshoes, and the Beta Company has been making horseshoe nails.

Since structure matches value, the sentence is unified. The sentence is disunified if you say

> John sold 50 shares of Ajax Can and Ajax Can is the world's largest maker of trout flies.

To make the relationship clear, you could say it this way:

> Since demand for trout flies has fallen off sharply, John sold his 50 shares of Ajax Can, world's largest producer of these artificial lures.

The main idea (John sold the shares) is expressed in the main clause. The subordinate idea about lowered demand is expressed in a subordinate construction, while the identification of Ajax as a producer of artificial flies is made in an appositive construction attached to the main clause.

When you are having trouble with a sentence, try writing out all the ideas in simple sentences. Then think about the relationship of the various ideas. Hunt a construction that best serves your intended meaning. If you cannot find one, you are probably trying to pack too much into a single sentence. Simplify—remember?

Here is one attempt to show relationships among the ideas expressed in simple sentences earlier:

> John felt he needed to look over his investments. Of special concern were his 50 shares of Ajax Can, a leading producer of trout lures. But too few people were trout fishing anymore. They were turning to horsebackriding by the thousands. If John wanted to salvage his money, he'd have to move it into something more promising. Something connected with horses would be ideal. Then, he discovered Alpha-Beta, a new company. It had been created out of a merger of two old-line companies who knew everything about making horseshoes and horseshoe nails. The company was in an excellent position to profit from the recreational market's new interest. John sold Ajax Can and bought Alpha-Beta.

Now it is readable and not at all stuffy. But it is choppy and juvenile. Let's try again.

> Because John owned 50 shares of Ajax Can, a producer of trout lures, he was concerned about the public's shift in interest from fishing to horse-backriding. Searching for companies that might profit from the trend, he discovered Alpha-Beta, a company with experience in making horse-shoes and horseshoe nails. After careful investigation, he decided to sell his interest in Ajax Can and to invest in Alpha-Beta.

The passage will not win any prizes for gracefulness and precision, but it is a start. Relationships are clear, sentences are unified, and the version might do for many purposes.

In all revisions, you gain something and you lose something. Jacques Barzun said it and it is true: "Simple English is nobody's mother tongue." To get a passage the way you want it is miserable, hard work. Frequently, though, it is absolutely necessary.

Fat Sentences

Sentences that accumulate too much detail grow fat. Put qualifying thoughts in separate sentences when you can do it without being choppy and without giving them more emphasis than they logically deserve. As a rule of thumb, do not let subordinate elements run to more than one-third of a sentence. Try not to let a subordinate element run over 10 words. Sentences in management writing should average about 20 words—or fewer. Have some longer ones, of course, but hold the average down. And don't be mechanical or slavish about any of these simplifications. (See section 25, "How to Make Your Writing Complete, Concise, and Easy to Read.")

Faulty Sentence Fragments

To be complete, a sentence should have a subject and a verb and any necessary modifiers. A construction lacking a subject or a verb is called a sentence fragment. While not all sentence fragments are bad, you should avoid using them unless you have a special effect in mind. A fragment sometimes lightens the tone of a passage and, carefully phrased, can ease reading. If by using a fragment you can accomplish these desirable goals and be perfectly clear in spite of the missing words, don't hesitate to put one in now and then. Used habitually, the technique defeats its purpose.

> INEFFECTIVE: The president said he will veto the emergency energy legislation that passed Congress Wednesday. *Rolling back crude oil prices.* The bill, he said, would lead to longer lines at the gas pumps.
>
> EFFECTIVE (maybe): Auto makers would be allowed a two-year delay in meeting exhaust standards. *Another defeat for the environmentalists.*

Choppy Sentences

Choppy sentences result when a writer treats all his ideas as equally important and uses similar structures and lengths to express them.

> I formulated a hypothesis. Then I drew up a questionnaire. I sent the questionnaire to 1,000 people. I tabulated the replies I got. I interpreted the replies. I checked my interpretation against my hypothesis. I revised my hypothesis somewhat. I began to write my report.

Choppy writing is bad enough, but it is not the worst kind of writing in the world. It is better to be choppy and clear than to be fluent and unclear.

Faulty Coordination and Subordination

The world presents itself to the senses in coordinate sequence or simultaneously. A leaf is as important as a steam engine. An ant is as significant as a hurricane. Two men walk down the street. The clock strikes eleven. Clouds hang low on the valley. Cars circle the parking area. A dog barks. But the mind is not satisfied with an avalanche of equal impressions. It keeps insisting that for each situation some things are more important than others, and it finds ways to express the relative importance of phenomena. Nobody needs the writer as a source of unrelated data. The world supplies data very well. The writer is needed to show how one idea depends on another.

Coordination is easy enough. Similar sentence patterns joined by the word *and* show coordination:

> Oil is scarce and taxes are high.

The word *but* also indicates that the ideas joined are of equal importance:

> Cuban cigars taste better, but American cigars are cheaper.

How one idea contributes to the importance of another is a little more difficult to express in writing:

> Since American cigars do not taste so good as Cuban cigars, they are not sought after and are therefore cheaper.

Faults in Parallel Structure

To show that one idea is as valuable as another or that one idea functions as strongly as another, put both in similar structures. Use words like *and, but, or, nor, for* to join like elements—clause to clause, phrase to phrase, word to word. Similar structure helps the reader understand the worth of the parts. The best way to see the value of parallel structure is to examine sentences without it.

> If you hire this man, you can be sure he will be honest, won't be hard to teach, and would stick by you in a crisis.

In this sentence not only does the tense shift but the reasons also switch from positive to negative. The reader can work out the intended meaning, but it takes some effort. The sentence is improved by putting the reasons in structures of similar value.

> If you hire this man, you can be sure he will not lie or cheat, will not resist job training, and will not desert you in a crisis.

Now the elements are parallel, but the sentence suffers somewhat from the need to state the reasons negatively. Let's try again.

> If you hire this man, you can be sure he will be honest, able, and loyal.

Now it is parallel, short, and crisp, but it lacks the specific impact of the one before it. Can we have positive statement, specific detail, *and* compactness? Let's try one more time.

> If you hire this man, you can be sure he will give you a fair day's work, will learn his job quickly, and will be loyal in a crisis.

Here are some more examples of faulty parallel structures, followed by suggested revisions. Before looking at the revision, try to improve the faulty sentence yourself by putting it into parallel form. Fortunately, parallelism is habit forming. If you practice, you'll get good at it.

> FAULTY: Excessive greed and being too lazy are common faults of otherwise competent people.

Since *greed* is a noun and *lazy* is an adjective, they do not link gracefully.

> IMPROVED: Greed and laziness are common faults of otherwise competent people.

Now try this one, keeping in mind that items in a series should be parallel:

> FAULTY: Mr. Ushiba has three very strong qualifications: a good education, he works hard, and intelligence.
>
> IMPROVED: Mr. Ushiba has three strong qualifications: He is well educated; he is industrious; he is intelligent.

Notice how repeating *he is* in the sentence helps establish parallelism.

Since lists are easy to read, you will want to use them to offer items in series. However, when you do, be sure all items in the list are expressed in similar constructions.

> The training director is responsible to the industrial relations manager for the following duties:
> managing the apprentice program
> conducting the orientation program for new employees
> scheduling interviews with employees leaving the company
> acting as associate editor of the house organ
> serving as secretary of the safety committee.

Be careful when using *and which, but which, and who,* and *and that.* The conjunctions *and* and *but* should be used before a relative clause only when that clause follows another relative clause referring to the same antecedent. In other words, the *and* or *but* can connect a clause to a clause but should not connect a clause to a phrase or to a word. It might help to think of *and* or *but* as a pivot point. For the parallelism to work, the construction, but not necessarily the length, on one side of the scale must match the construction on the opposite side.

> FAULTY: The auditor picked up a second volume, a much larger one than the first, and which contained all the accounts of the company's first year.
>
> IMPROVED: The auditor picked up a second volume which was much larger than the first and which contained all the accounts of the company's first year.

Now, the *and* connects clause to clause (which to which) and not word to clause as in the faulty version.

Faulty *and which, and that, and who,* and *but which* constructions can often be improved by recasting to avoid the problem entirely.

> FAULTY: He knows more about hay balers than any other man alive and which is responsible for his department's fine record.
>
> IMPROVED: His superior knowledge of hay balers makes him responsible for his department's fine record.
>
> FAULTY: Hiram is a splendid salesman and who knows more about hay balers than anybody else.
>
> IMPROVED: Hiram is a splendid salesman who knows more about hay balers than anybody else.

Don't forget that comparisons also require parallel forms. While you have no need to compare identical things, you often compare two similar things that have some definite differences. Something is bigger than something else. Something is more difficult to do than something else. The word to watch for is *than*. When you write it, you may be about to make a comparison. If so, be careful. Comparing someone to yourself is particularly tricky—grammatically, that is, and probably psychologically as well. Frequently, the second part of a comparison is abbreviated or implied, and the comparison is stated illogically.

> ILLOGICAL: Wilcox makes more money than me.

You will write it correctly if you remember to mentally supply the implied word or words.

> LOGICAL: Wilcox makes more money than I [make].

Here is another comparison. Remember that parallel thoughts require parallel structure.

> ILLOGICAL: Directing the work of others requires more skill than a carpenter.

Directing is an activity. A carpenter is a person. How can the two things be compared? They can't. Like things must be compared in like structures.

> LOGICAL: A supervisor needs more skill than a carpenter [needs].

Now, a person is compared to a person. Structures are similar.

> LOGICAL: Supervising requires more skill than carpentering.

Two human activities, supervising and carpentering, are compared in similar structures. The comparison is logically phrased.

However, notice that grammatical logic does not guarantee the truth of a statement. Merely stating, even in logical grammar, that a supervisor needs more skill than a carpenter does not make it so. Maybe carpenters need more skill. Maybe the skill each needs can't logically be compared. Maybe it doesn't matter. What does matter is that you remember that putting words in logical structures does not absolve you of responsibility for what the words are saying.

Dangling Modifiers

Sometimes, in constructing a sentence beginning with a participle, a gerund, or an infinitive, a writer will forget what noun the phrase should point to. If it relates to the wrong one, the modifier dangles, often with the same kind of ludicrous image that results from pinning the tail on the wrong end of the donkey. We can easily recognize the obvious ones like "Flying through the air and emitting loud whoops, my husband saw a crane" or "Swinging through the trees I saw a monkey." Usually the dangler is not so ridiculous and the reader has no trouble finding the intended meaning.

> Roaring down the track in one final cloud of dust, the race ended in victory for Rod Sparks.

Check, in rough draft, all *ing* phrases and all infinitive phrases (*to have, to make,* etc.) to be certain that the noun following the phrase is the one logically referred to in the phrase.

> FAULTY (dangling participle): Running a grave risk of a lawsuit against him, the contract was nevertheless changed.
>
> IMPROVED: Running a grave risk of a lawsuit against him, he nevertheless changed the contract.
>
> FAULTY (dangling gerund): After changing the wording in the offending document, the contract was filed in the security box.
>
> IMPROVED: After he changed the wording in the offending document, he filed the contract in the security box.
>
> FAULTY (Dangling infinitive): To succeed in business, iron nerves, a strong stomach, and a tough behind are needed.
>
> IMPROVED: To succeed in business, one must have iron nerves, a strong stomach, and a tough behind.

Most danglers come from the writer's habit of making constructions in the passive voice. Keep the *doer* of the act in mind and avoid danglers.

Some expressions are so commonly used that even though they dangle they are acceptable.

> Generally speaking, the air in Arizona is less humid than the air in Pennsylvania.

Although the air is not speaking, the meaning is clear.

Misplaced Modifiers

If a word or a phrase is not placed next to the noun it should modify, it will modify the noun it is placed next to. Sometimes such a misplacement can seriously distort a writer's intention. Since most sentences have a few nouns, it is very easy to get a modifier hanging onto the wrong noun—like a child in a crowd who takes a stranger's hand thinking it is his father's. Is it clear, in the preceding sentence, that *who* refers to child? Since it follows *crowd,* the reader for a moment is not sure. He realizes at once that a crowd cannot take a stranger's hand and he is not too upset. Still, it would be better to recast:

> like a child who, bemused in a crowd, takes a stranger's hand thinking it is his father's.

Most misplaced modifiers are like this one, mildly bothersome to a reader, but not embarrassing to a writer. Some, usually the ones chosen to illustrate a textbook, are not so benign because they carry a bonus to the reader (and onus to the writer) of unintended humor. It can happen to anybody. Be careful.

FAULTY: He almost was late for every appointment that week.

IMPROVED: He was late for almost every appointment that week.

FAULTY: A man should never try to eat soup with a mustache.

IMPROVED: A man with a mustache should never try to eat soup.

FAULTY: Earrings are not recommended for small women with more than one pendulous globe.

IMPROVED: Earrings with more than one pendulous globe are not recommended for small women.

Squinting Modifiers

Sometimes a modifier sits in a pivot position from which it can modify two elements at the same time. Because such modifiers look both ways, they are called "squinting." If the sentence is read with a certain inflection, it will mean one thing. If read with a different emphasis, it will mean another. Often both possibilities make sense and the reader is confused. Put the modifier where it can look at only what it is supposed to look at.

FAULTY: People who change jobs frequently don't investigate the community they will move to.

IMPROVED: Frequently, people who change jobs don't investigate the community they will move to.

Faulty Reference of Pronouns

A pronoun stands for a noun. Make certain the reader has no doubt which noun a pronoun refers to.

FAULTY: The Yankees beat the Indians yesterday, but they didn't play so well as they usually do.

IMPROVED: The Yankees beat the Indians yesterday, possibly because the Indians didn't play so well as they usually do.

IMPROVED: Although the Yankees didn't play so well as they usually do, they beat the Indians yesterday.

Remote Antecedent

If you use *it* or *this* to refer to a noun or to an idea, check that the position of the pronoun does not fall so far behind the noun it refers to that the reader will no longer remember the reference point.

FAULTY: Some Duffield sandy loam is found along the northwest slope of Warrior Ridge where the sandy Dekalb soil material from higher levels has been carried down and deposited on the Duffield soils that occupy the slopes below the Dekalb soils, thereby giving rise to a sandy loam surface soil that rests on the silt and clay over the underlying silty limestones. *This* differs from Duffield silt loam, rolling phase, only in texture of the surface soil.

IMPROVED: Duffield sandy loam differs from Duffield silt loam only in texture of the surface soil.

Vague References

To avoid vague references, try to make a pronoun refer to a specific noun and not to a general idea or to the idea of a whole sentence.

FAULTY: Japan can be expected to maintain an alliance with the United States, but under a revised treaty. This may or may not be satisfactory.

The reader is not sure what the writer intends to say. Could it be unsatisfactory to maintain an alliance? If so, for whom? Or does the writer mean a revised treaty may be unsatisfactory?

IMPROVED: Japan can be expected to maintain an alliance with the United States, but under a revised treaty. Such a treaty may or may not be satisfactory to the United States.

Shifts in Point of View

In general, keep your viewpoint consistent in person, tense, voice, number, tone, and objectivity.

Person

For most business letter writing, use first person (I, we) and second person (you) points of view. Using these forms, where people are the doers, keeps the tone immediate. Choose the *you* form whenever you want to involve the reader and appeal to his interests. In reports, your audience and the circumstances often demand the more formal tone of the third person.

Make a point of keeping person consistent throughout a passage. Sudden shifts disconcert the reader. If you are writing a report in the first person and switch to the third, the reader will wonder why. Look at this passage that shifts from third to second person:

> A business writer should have a good ear for language. If you do not, your sentences will always be slightly off key.

To be consistent, this writer should choose a person and stick with it throughout the passage. Since his intention is to keep his writing immediate, he recasts the first sentence into the second person.

> As a business writer, you should have a good ear for language. If you do not, your sentences will always be slightly off key.

Now the passage is both immediate and consistent. Perhaps, though, it is a bit too personal for the circumstances. If our writer fears offending his reader by seeming to point an accusing finger, he might well decide to shift the entire passage into the third person.

> A business writer should have a good ear for language. If he does not, his sentences will always be slightly off key.

Tense

Proofread your rough drafts carefully to be certain you have avoided unnecessary changes in tense.

> FAULTY: Earnings per share of common stock exceeded the program by a wide margin in November. Although profit before taxes was substantially below program, profit after taxes are considerably above.
>
> IMPROVED: . . . profit before taxes was substantially below program, profit after taxes was considerably above.

Voice

Verbs have two voices, active and passive. The active voice is just that—active. It highlights the *agent of the action* that the verb names. Therefore, the active voice has a built-in force and directness that the passive voice lacks. Naturally, then, for crisp, lively sentences, you will want to use the active voice whenever possible.

Choose the passive voice when the doer of the activity is less important than the fact that something was done. Sometimes, writers use the passive voice to suppress responsibility for actions. For example, the teenager who has borrowed the family car might well choose the passive form

The car was wrecked.

rather than the more bold

I wrecked the car.

Unless you have a sufficient reason for choosing the passive form, use the active voice to keep your sentences vigorous and your intentions straightforward.

FAULTY: A team of researchers at New Appliance developed an apple picker that could actually climb a tree and sense the presence of an apple. The apple was removed from the stem and deposited in an opening in the machine's side.

Why does the writer shift attention from the picker to the apple? Since there is not a sufficient reason for him to do so, he should recast to maintain point of view.

IMPROVED: The picker could climb a tree, sense an apple, remove the apple from the stem, and deposit it in a container.

Number

Don't confuse the reader by changing from singular to plural or vice versa in a sentence.

FAULTY: Everyone should punch their own card.
IMPROVED: Everyone should punch his own card.

Tone

Do not switch tone. If the writing is serious, keep it that way throughout.

> American men and women who have served in the uniforms of their country may have items of historical interest that should be preserved for posterity. Personal papers and letters, diaries, photographs, souvenirs, and crap like that may have interest later in scholarly research.

It is not hard to see which phrase violates the tone of that statement.

Objectivity

In addition to a change in tone, the following passage shows a shift in objectivity. From what seemed to be a reasoned, responsible, objective opinion, we see a sudden shift to personal bias.

> It is not likely that the present oil shortage will seriously affect the value of rural real estate. Cities will continue to suffer air pollution, probably at an accelerated rate; increasing population will make movement to the country necessary; and there will always be the nature freaks and the boondockers who don't realize that nature is the real enemy.

Mixed Constructions

Business writing must usually be done quickly. It must be clear, but it need not be beautiful. In the haste of making a rough draft, it is easy to create a mixed construction. This fault occurs often in dictation—an ending and a beginning that do not quite match. Revision is in order.

> FAULTY: Whenever separated columns would be so narrow they would be difficult to draw is a good time to leave out spaces between them.
>
> IMPROVED: If you do not have enough room to separate columns, don't try to. Just leave out the space between the columns.

Faulty Emphasis

Arrange items in a series so that the most important item comes at the end and there is logical progression.

FAULTY: He is guilty of every crime in the books: rape, tax evasion, murder, shoplifting, car theft, and sneaking into football games without a ticket.

IMPROVED: . . . sneaking into football games without a ticket, shoplifting, tax evasion, car theft, rape, and murder.

Know when to use the loose sentence and when to use the periodic sentence. In the periodic sentence the strong or conclusive statement is saved for the end. In the loose sentence the essential point is offered early and additional material later. If the essential point is not especially dramatic and the qualifying material is almost as interesting, the loose sentence is satisfactory.

Elmer learned self-reliance as a child growing up in a log cabin tucked away in the foothills of West Virginia where loneliness taught a boy how to look out for himself.

It would not do to build up too much suspense to deliver the information that Elmer learned self-reliance.

If you are going to use the periodic sentence, make sure that the information you are saving for the end is worth it. Here is an ineffective example of this construction:

After a series of setbacks, not the least of which was the fire that destroyed the main building, and then a disheartening lawsuit that forbade his rebuilding it, Elmer lost three golf balls.

Unless the golf balls were studded with diamonds, it would be better to announce their loss in a less dramatic way. The following example demonstrates a more valid use of the periodic construction:

One fateful day in the closing months of World War II the plane I was to take to London (but which I missed because of a cab driver's error) crashed and burned on takeoff.

Lifeless Sentences

Sentences weighed down by unnecessary words are lifeless. Make nouns and verbs work for you. Begin by restricting your use of adjectives and adverbs. So that you can emphasize the doer, resist using the passive voice. Pay particular attention to sentences that start with *there* and *it*. Often, these words are used thoughtlessly by a writer who is merely warming to his subject. Frequently, he is halfway into the sentence before he delivers the message, as the following examples illustrate:

> FAULTY: There will be a meeting of the Organic Food Club in the Fire Hall at 8:00 P.M.
>
> IMPROVED: The Organic Food Club will meet. . . .
>
> FAULTY: There will be a reduction in the sales force at the River installation this spring.
>
> IMPROVED: The River installation will reduce its sales force this spring.

Practice lively sentences by writing the significant noun first. Follow it with an active verb. Then add necessary qualifiers. Soon you will break the lifeless sentence habit.

SECTION 30

How to Choose the Right Word

Level of Usage

The language appropriate to business writing is a dialect called Standard English. It may not be your mother tongue. It is the acquired language of educated people wherever English is used. It is not superior to any other dialect. It has value because it serves a purpose. It can be understood in Melbourne and Minneapolis, in Austin and Anchorage, in Cape Town and Charlestown. Other dialects of English have been formed on geographic, ethnic, or social lines. (In Lancaster County, Pennsylvania, one can speak of plain people and gay people and natives will know that *plain* refers to Amish and Mennonite people who dress uniformly in usually dark clothing without frills and that *gay* refers to people who dress in response to style changes in order to be attractive or interesting—or at least for more complicated reasons than just to keep covered and warm. In other territory the words *plain* and *gay* may have different meanings.) But Standard English is universal. Therefore, anyone who wants to move easily in the world of daily intercourse must learn Standard English.

Two levels of Standard English affect the business writer—the formal level and the informal level. There are levels of usage in business writing just as in other forms of communication. Although the predominant value is informal, times occur when a formal tone is appropriate. Much business writing is relaxed and personalized, but the breezy letter, the sarcastic memo, or the slangy report is wisely avoided. Humor may work where it is least expected—as in a collection letter—but it frequently backfires. Clear, direct, simple English is the objective.

Invented Words

Nor is "Darrow" any longer just the name of a man. It has now entered the mainstream of the American language, and soon will be in the dictionaries. On radio, television and in the press I have heard it used as a noun, an adjective and an adverb. "What do you think you are, a Darrow?" "That was a very Darrowesque approach." "Their lawyer is very Darrow-like."

—Irving Stone

Mr. Stone may be right about *Darrow.* Words are made that way. But the careful writer does not pick them up too readily. They often irritate. Words, like shoes or pipes, are more comfortable after they have been broken in. For every new word that serves well and makes a place for itself, there are dozens of barbarous inventions that never make the team—or should not. Notice some of the atrocities that have entered the language on the heels of *feasance,* from Anglo-French *fesance* and French *faire,* "to do." We get *feasible* out of that, and it does a decent job ("That is a feasible explanation"). But we also get *malfeasance,* which means doing something bad. Some people have used *malfeasor* to identify the person who has done a bad thing. Then comes *nonfeasance,* which means doing nothing one should do, and one who does nothing is a *nonfeasor* ("He was fired for nonfeasance"). It seems that everybody is a *feasor* of some type or other. ("How do you fease today?" "Hardly able to fease at all, thank you.") And we forgot *misfeasance,* which is doing something you should not do, not necessarily bad, which of course makes you a *misfeasor.* Arrgh.

Connotation and Denotation

Denotation is the specific meaning of or the object designated by a word apart from any emotional coloring the word suggests. Connotation is the suggestive or the associative significance the word calls out in addition to the literal meaning or the actual object. *Domicile, home, house, residence,* all denote a structure in which people might live. One sees a roof, a hearth, an address number, some sort of composite of all the apartments or houses one knows. Connotations differ, however. The words are not interchangeable. *Dog, cur, mongrel, whelp, pooch* have similar denotations but rather different connotations. "The violinist was walking his dog around the block" has respectable connotations. "The fiddler hoofed it around the block with his pooch" has unpleasant connotations.

In business writing be careful of innuendo, of connotation. The business writer sticks close to the denotative side of words. Richness of connotation is not a virtue in business writing.

Catchall Words

Catchall words are wild words, that is, they can be used by the author to stand for any other word in the language. With them it is sometimes possible to speak for five minutes and not say anything. They are useful in hiding an idea or hiding the fact that there *is* no idea. Some wild words are *field, factor, circumstance, aspect, thing, case, point, situation, type, respect* (n.).

> In some respects a valid point could be made that this thing is a factor in the situation, some aspect of which will surely come home to haunt us if a point is not made soon to alter the circumstance.

Save these words for desperate circumstances, where being clear would be dead wrong.

Figures of Speech

The most common figures of speech are the *simile*—a comparison using the word *like,* as in "He fought like a tiger"—and the *metaphor,* in which the writer compares one thing to another not by saying it is *like* the other but by saying it *is* the other: "Wilson was a tiger in the ring tonight." In daily speech, figures come as naturally as breathing, and they enliven language. They can be effective in writing, too, but there they need some thought. It is better not to show off with them, as in "We can short-circuit the electricity shortage if we don't fall asleep at the switch." Avoid trite figures, such as *fresh as a daisy* or *busy as a bee* (see "Trite and Wordy Expressions" later in this section). In addition, avoid mixed figures, which are confusing as well as careless.

> If we want this pipeline of contracts to stay open we had better keep our heads down and not make waves until this bottleneck gets ironed out.

The mind boggles trying to sort out the images.

Directness

Do not waste words. In all messages there should be balance between intention and tone. Words used should be appropriate to the intention of the writer and to his view of what the reader needs. Brevity is not always the primary value. "Thank you for the gift" is direct and brief, but hardly ever an adequate reply. More should be said. About how the gift will be used; how it matches some other prized possession; how it pleases other people. Whatever is added to the message, however, should be said directly and economically. The following message is not direct:

> In the interest of clarification, the procedure for scheduling flights in company aircraft is furnished for your information and guidance. Authorization for use and availability of company aircraft must be obtained from the traffic officer. As the designated scheduling agency for all flights involving company aircraft, except those originating in the president's office, the traffic officer will obtain proper authorization and clearance prior to making any firm commitment for transportation. It is requested that department heads ensure coordination with the visitors bureau prior to making any commitment of company aircraft to transport guests to and from the premises. Such coordination will preclude the occurrence of possibly embarrassing and awkward situations in making transportation arrangements for the many distinguished guests of the company.

A more direct message might be

> To avoid embarrassment please check with the traffic officer before you promise your guest transportation in company aircraft.

"Fine Writing"

"Fine writing" is writing intended to impress the reader rather than to inform him. It is characterized by flowery adjectives and "elegant variations" of verbs and nouns. It comes from the mistaken notion that simple is easy and somehow beneath the dignity of a high-level person. (See section 25, "How to Make Your Writing Complete, Concise, and Easy to Read.")

Euphemisms

Certain words have unpleasant overtones. They are felt to be coarse or blunt, or they remind us of our mortality, of our low station in life, or some other misfortune. A euphemism is a substitute word that is felt to convey less pain or in some way to diminish the unpleasantness of the ordinary word.

COMMON TERM	EUPHEMISM
die	pass away
syphilis	social disease
janitor	maintenance engineer
old man	senior citizen
drunk	intoxicated
backward nation	developing nation
loafer	underachiever
undertaker	mortician
fat	portly

If the only way you can avoid giving offense to a reader is to use a euphemism, use it. But do not give in without a struggle. You can usually find a direct expression. Certainly *poor* is less patronizing than *disadvantaged*.

Trite and Wordy Expressions

Your value to an organization comes from your ability to see reality with fresh insight and to explain your truth in fresh language. The trouble with a trite expression is that it has lost its power to evoke surprise or wonder. It's a prefabricated phrase that leaps into your sentence so that you will be able to go on writing without thinking. The question comes up: How do we handle the enemy? The answer is already worded, ready to be slipped into the opening: "We will close with the enemy and destroy his will to fight." What must we do to gain support of the people? "We must win their hearts and minds." How much force shall we use? "Only the degree of force that is necessary." What shall we press for? "Unconditional surrender." What will we settle for? "Peace with honor."

Often no harm comes from using ready-made expressions. Approximations to your genuine thought are sometimes good enough. You can't invent fresh language for *everything* you say. But most of the time you should reject, at least at first, the trite expression and ask yourself what you really think. The problem, though old, may have new complications, and your fresh insight and fresh language may simplify it. If you can't think of a fresh way of expressing your thought, don't try to escape responsibility by putting the cliché in quotes. Just use it.

Three lists of some common clichés and wordy expressions follow. Some expressions on the lists are less harmful than others: They do not represent any particular evasion of thought. Reject them because they are tired, wordy, and ineffective.

CLICHES IN GENERAL USE

abreast of the times	bolt from the blue
acid test	bountiful repast
a few well-chosen words	breakneck speed
agree to disagree	break the news gently
almighty dollar	budding genius
among those present	but that's another story
at one fell swoop	by leaps and bounds
bated breath	captain of industry
beat a hasty retreat	center of attraction
beg to say	checkered career
best-laid plans	commercial pursuits

CLICHES IN GENERAL USE (CONT.)

conspicuous by his absence
day of reckoning
die is cast
doomed to disappointment
down through the ages
each and every one
endorse the sentiments
equal to the occasion
every walk of life
exception that proves the
  rule
fast and furious
goes without saying
gone but not forgotten
greatness thrust upon
his paternal (maternal)
  ancestor
host of friends
impenetrable mystery
in any way, shape, or form
irony of fate
last but not least
looking for all the world like
lull before the storm

made a pronounced success
misguided youth
nipped in the bud
no sooner said than done
perfect in every detail
powers that be
profound silence
psychological moment
riot of color
ripe old age
sadder but wiser
seething mass of humanity
silence reigned supreme
skeleton in the closet
the scene beggars
  description
vale of tears
venture a suggestion
veritable avalanche
view with alarm
work like a Trojan
words are inadequate
words fail me
worse for wear

CLICHES COMMON IN BUSINESS

according to our records
acknowledge receipt of
allow me to state
and oblige
as per your request
assuring you of our prompt
  attention
at all times
at hand
attached please find
at this time
awaiting your favor
awaiting your further orders
beg to state
by return mail
contents duly noted
dictated but not read
enclosed herewith
enclosed please find

esteemed favor
even date
favor (as a synonym for
  letter)
for your information
has come to hand
in due course
keep our options open
recent date
same (as pronoun to stand
  for noun in previous sentence)
Thanking you in advance
the undersigned
this letter is for the purpose
under separate cover
we wish to advise
we would ask that
would state
you claim, you say, you state

WORDY EXPRESSIONS WITH SUGGESTIONS FOR REPHRASING

Instead of	*Try to use*
abovementioned	this, these
after very careful consideration	after considering
ahead of schedule	early
along the lines of	like
apropos of the above	regarding, concerning
at such time	when
attached you will find	attached is
at your earliest convenience	soon, immediately, as quickly as possible
comes into conflict	conflicts
despite the fact that	even though, although
due in large measure to	due largely
due to the fact that	because
each of these	each
enclosed herewith is	enclosed is
for the purpose of	for
for the reason that	since
give consideration to	consider
give encouragement to	encourage
give instruction to	instruct
give rise to	cause
have need for	need
if doubt is entertained	if doubtful
in a most careful manner	carefully
in accordance with	by
in a satisfactory manner	satisfactorily
inasmuch as	as
in the amount of	for
in the event that	if
in the case of	if
in the near future	soon
in view of the foregoing	therefore, hence, as, because
is of the opinion	believes
in large measure	largely
make inquiry regarding	inquire
make an adjustment in	adjust
of the order of magnitude	about
on the basis of	by, from
on the occasion of	on
of a confidential nature	confidential
owing to the fact that	because
prior to	before
subsequent to	after
take into consideration	consider

How to Control Troublesome Expressions

This book has been concerned with the reasons people have for hating to write. They hate to write because they lack interest in their subject; they don't especially care to influence a reader. They'd rather use the telephone. What they write may come back to haunt them. But one reason they hate to write is this: No matter how much care they take, there will certainly be the reader somewhere who will look at the letter, memo, or report and say, "You said it wrong. You wrote *enthused* and that isn't even a word. You dummy."

For that reason, the list that follows is presented with reluctance. It's a list that seems to go on forever showing examples of your favorite expressions, expressions that turn out to be much objected to by the guardians of Standard English, especially by that insufferable snob referred to again and again as "the purist." You'll get to hate them and him unless you go about the whole list with good humor, or at least a bit of tolerance. Worry about correctness is an emotion most likely to keep a blank page blank.

Recommendation: Get the rough draft. Say it your way. To hell with the purist, this book, your English teacher, and Edwin Newman. Get it down. But after you get the rough draft, after you've asserted yourself, you must in all fairness to your intention wonder if your satisfaction is the only consideration. Now you have a product before you. Will it do its job? What will others say about it? How will your audience respond? Will what you have written do what you want it to do?

For your writing to succeed, you must know the conventions, the etiquette, the biases about language held by the community you work in, your colleagues, your clients, your boss. Then, armed with knowledge, you can choose the forms you want for the effect you want.

The following list [1] is intended to inform you of the status of various terms and expressions. Read the arguments; then do what you

---

1. We are indebted to Christian K. Arnold for many of the items on this list.

like, remembering that you are responsible for what you say and how you say it.

ability, capacity   *Ability* means "the power to do something." *Capacity* means "the power to receive or to hold."

> Winston has the ability [*not* the capacity] to type eighty words a minute.

about, approximately   *Approximately* suggests an attempt at calculation of accuracy; *about* makes no such suggestion.

> The water content is approximately 25 percent by volume.
> It is about twenty miles to Black Moshannon Mountain.

above   An adverb, although widely used as an adjective.

> ADVERBIAL USE: as stated above
> ADJECTIVAL USE: the above remark

Purists consider its adjectival use to be inelegant and inaccurate. *Foregoing* and *preceding* are acceptable synonyms.

accept, except   *Accept* means "to agree to receive"; *except* means "to exclude." Don't use *except* in the sense of *unless,* as in "We will not send the material except you send the cash."

adequate enough   This phrase is redundant, since it says the same thing twice. Omit either *adequate* or *enough.* See **Redundancy.**

admit, confess   Admit a truth. Confess a fault. *Admit* also means "to allow to pass," as in "Please admit the bearer of this card to the meeting."

adverse, averse   *Adverse* means "antagonistic" or "strongly opposed." *Averse* means "unwilling."

advise   *Advise* means "to give counsel or advice." It is jargon when used as a substitute for *say, tell, inform,* etc. Avoid using *advise* in this sense. *Beg to advise* is both stilted and trite. See **Jargon.**

> He told [*not* advised] us that the test was a success.

affect, effect   *Affect* is a verb meaning "to change or influence."

> How do you think the oil shortage will affect the value of rural property?

Effect is a noun meaning "result or outcome."

> What is the effect of the oil shortage on the value of rural property?

Effect is also a verb meaning "to bring about."

> The president was not able to effect a change in the policy.

aggravate *Aggravate* means "to make worse."

> Travel in the country often aggravates a sinus condition.

Don't use it as a synonym for *annoy* or *provoke*, as in "His greediness aggravates me."

agree to, agree with One agrees *to* a plan but *with* a person. One thing agrees *with* another.

> The president agreed to the outlined sales program.
> The vice president agreed with the president.
> Our experimental results agreed with the sales manager's theory.

a half an hour Substandard. Use *half an hour* or *a half hour*.

all of The *of* in this expression is redundant. Omit *of* except when it is followed by a pronoun, where its use is accepted. See **Redundancy.**

> All work [*not* all of the work] was completed.
> All of us want to go to the convention in Key West.

all over A provincial expression used to mean "everywhere" or "throughout an area."

> Dandelions are found everywhere [*not* all over].

allow Use it in the sense of *permit* but not in the sense of *admit* or *think.*

> He thought [*not* allowed] the price was high.

all the farther, all the higher, etc. Such expressions are incorrect substitutes for *as far as, as high as,* etc. Also see **farther, further.**

> This is as far as [*not* all the farther] we went.

along this line, along the lines of These phrases have been so overworked, especially in technical writing, that they have become trite and practically meaningless. Their use should be avoided whenever possible. *Along the lines of least resistance* is especially threadbare.

> NOT: He said nothing further along these lines.
> BUT: He did not discuss it further.
>
> NOT: We proceeded along the lines of Detwiler's theory.
> BUT: We followed Detwiler's theory in our investigation.

alright For a long time, many considered *alright* to be an illiterate form of *all right.* The people who insist on *all right* seem to be losing ground, but you might want to avoid using *alright* until its acceptance is established. *All right,* now in good standing, earlier was considered a colloquial substitute for *very well.*

alumna, alumnae   Feminine singular and plural.

> She is an alumna of Vassar College.
> Ruth and Betty are alumnae of Vassar.

alumnus, alumni   Masculine singular and plural.

> He is an alumnus of Yale University.
> George and Ralph are alumni of Duke University.

Used to refer collectively to graduates of both sexes, *alumni* now has sexist connotations; *graduates* is a better choice.

amateur, novice   An amateur is not a professional. He is not necessarily a beginner and he may be quite skillful. A novice is a beginner.

among   See **between.**

amount, number   Use *amount* to refer to a mass, a bulk, or a sum.

> There is a large amount of coal in the valley.

Use *number* to refer to a collection that can be counted.

> The library has a large number of books.

This distinction also applies to *less* and *fewer;* see **fewer, less.**

ample opportunity   A much overworked phrase that is often carelessly allowed to stand in the place of a more accurate and forceful one. If *opportunity* needs to be modified, select a more meaningful and accurate adjective than the catchall *ample.*

and   Not an acceptable substitute for *to* in such expressions as "I'll try and find the answer." See **be sure and.**

and etc.   *Etc.* is the abbreviation for *et cetera,* Latin for "and others." Using *and* before *etc.* is equivalent to writing *and and others.* Obviously, the *and* should be omitted. Also see **etc.**

and moreover   Because *and* and *moreover* indicate the same kind of connection (addition), it is redundant to use them together. Omit one (usually *moveover*). See **Redundancy.**

and which, and who, and that   A common grammatical error consists of using an *and, but,* or *or* between an adjective clause introduced by *which, who,* or *that* and another modifier of a different sort. Do not use *and which, and who,* or *and that* unless there is a preceding *which, who,* or *that* clause, respectively modifying the same noun.

> NOT: We tested a second drill smaller than the first but which had a greater speed.
> BUT: We tested a second drill, which was smaller than the first but which was faster.
> OR: The second drill we tested was smaller than the first but faster.

See section 29, "How to Construct Good Sentences," under the heading *Faults in Parallel Structure.*

anxious   Avoid using as a synonym for *eager. Anxious* means "full of anxiety." If an event is looked forward to with pleasure, use *eager.*

> He was eager to go back to his home.

anywheres, nowheres, somewheres   Provincial for *anywhere, nowhere,* and *somewhere.*

appearing   Often a pretentious and unnecessarily formal substitute for the more natural *looking.*

> NOT: a comfortable-appearing house
> BUT: a comfortable-looking house

appraise, apprise   *Appraise* means "to determine the value of" or "to set a value on." *Apprise* means "to inform or notify."

> We must have the property appraised.
> The receptionist was not apprised of the fact.

approach   A vague and trite substitute for *speak to, ask, consult,* etc. Always select the simpler, more direct, and more accurate verb.

> NOT: We approached the plant manager about our plan.
> BUT: We consulted with [*or* conferred with] the plant manager about our plan.

approximately   See **about.**

apt   Means "ready to learn" or "a leaning toward some skill."

> He is an apt apprentice.

Play it safe. Don't use *apt* in place of *likely.*

> He is likely [*not* apt] to win the contest.

But remember—it's no big thing.

around   Colloquial when used in place of *about, in this vicinity,* or *about the time of.* Avoid using in these senses in formal writing.

Snow will fall about [*not* around] the first of December.
The inspectors will be in this area [*not* around here] tomorrow.
The test was started about [*not* around] two hours ago.

as   Avoid *as* whenever *because, since,* or *for* might be a better choice.

Because [*not* as] I was low in cash, I decided to give up breakfast.

Don't use *as* in place of *that* or *whether.*

I do not know that [*not* as] the company can reimburse you.

The correlatives *so . . . as* are preferred to *as . . . as* in negative sentences.

The chemical stocks are not quite so volatile as the plastic stocks.

ascetic, aesthetic   *Ascetic* means "austere," "abstemious." *Aesthetic* means "pertaining to or appreciative of beauty."

as far as . . . is concerned   At worst, this phrase is pure jargon. At best, it is a roundabout way of qualifying a statement that could almost always be qualified more directly and simply.

NOT: He made little progress as far as the design of the shopping mall is concerned.

This sentence implies more than it says and leaves many doubts in the mind of the reader.

BUT: He made little progress on the design of the shopping mall.
OR: His shopping mall design was a failure.

as long as   A wordy substitute for *since* or *because.*

Since [*not* as long as] it must be done, we might as well start.

aspect   A catchall word, easily overworked or misused. See **Jargon.**

as per   Avoid. *Per* means "through," "by," or "by means of." See **per.**

NOT: as per your request, as per the report
BUT: as you requested, according to the report

assemble together   *Assemble* means "to bring together"; consequently, *together* in the phrase *assemble together* is redundant and should be omitted. *Together* is also unnecessary with *gather, collect, join, combine, unite, connect, link, associate,* and *consolidate,* each of which denotes "together."

asset   An overworked word for identifying something useful or desirable. The word retains a commercial connotation, and careful writers select one of its many substitutes for use in noncommercial contexts: *advantage, benefit, interest, help,* etc.

> The availability of many young scientists is an advantage [*not* asset] to the laboratory.

as to   Avoid in the sense of "with reference to," "concerning."

> NOT: He was not certain as to how much authority he had.
> BUT: He was uncertain about [*or* of] the extent of his authority.

awful, awfully   Colloquial for *very, very much, extremely;* rarely used even in informal writing. In formal writing *awful* is strictly used to mean "inspiring awe," "causing fear," or "full of awe."

averse   See **adverse**.

back of, in back of   Colloquial for *behind*. Better avoided in this sense.

> He was behind [*not* in back of] the fence.

bad, badly   *Bad* is an adjective with numerous meanings; check your dictionary. *Badly* is an adverb meaning "in a bad manner." It is often used incorrectly with *feel* and *look*.

> He feels bad [distressed, regretful].
> He looks bad [ill].
> He plays golf badly.

balance   Once acceptable only in business usage in the sense of *remainder, rest, residue*. Now this sense is gaining acceptance in general usage.

bank on   A colloquial expression. In formal writing, use *rely on*.

because of, due to   See **due to**.

being as, being that   Use *since* or *because*.

> Because [*not* being as] he was only fourteen, he couldn't join the army.

beside, besides   *Beside* means "by the side of." *Besides* means "in addition to."

> If you stand beside me on this issue, I'll stand beside you when you have trouble.
> There are other considerations besides money.

be sure and   Avoid this construction when a following verb specifies what is to be made sure. Also see **and**.

> NOT: Be sure and lock the file.
> BUT: Be sure to lock the file.

better than   Colloquial when used to mean "more than."

> More than [*not* better than] ten tests were made.

between, among   Generally use *between* when writing of two things and *among* when writing of three or more. Both these prepositions indicate collective relationships.

> between a pair of things, among a group of things

Between is sometimes used to show a relationship involving more than two when each relates individually to each of the others.

> a treaty between three nations

big, large, great   All share the meaning "above average in magnitude." Distinctions, however, are made in preferred usage. *Big* is used when reference is made to bulk, mass, weight, or volume. *Large* is used with nouns indicating dimensions, extent, quantity, or capacity. *Great* is now used almost entirely to connote eminence, distinction, or supremacy and is usually not applied to material things.

> a big [bulky, heavy] man, a big book, a big [loud] voice
> a large [tall, broad] man, a large state, a large number
> a great physicist, a great symphony

blame on, blame it on   Many regard the phrase *blame it on* as a crude construction.

> NOT: He blamed the loss on me.
> BUT: He blamed me for the loss.
>
> NOT: If the new manager fails, you can blame it on her husband.
> BUT: If the new manager fails, you can blame her husband.

both   Watch out for redundancies. See **Redundancy.**

> FAULTY: Both of the companies failed.
> IMPROVED: Both companies failed.

bound   Don't use *bound* in the sense of *resolved* or *determined.*

> I am determined [*not* bound] to do it.

bring, take   *Bring* is often used imprecisely for *take*. Both mean "to carry," but one denotes "to" and the other "from" some implied or specified place.

> NOT: Bring it from here to there.
> BUT: Take it from here to there.
> Bring it to here from there.

The distinction between *bring* and *take* is the same as that between *come* and *go*.

bunch   Colloquial for *several* or *a group*.

bust, busted   Slang. Dialect variations of *burst*. Don't use *bust* as a verb.

>   NOT: The balloon bust [*or* busted].
>   BUT: The balloon burst [*not* bursted *either*].

but nevertheless   This expression is redundant, since the two connectives indicate the same type of relation (opposition or contrast). Omit one of the words. See **Redundancy**.

but what, but that   Substitute *that*.

>   I have no doubt that [*not* but that *or* but what] he will sell the house.

calculate, reckon   Colloquial and dialectal in the sense of *think, suppose, guess*. Properly used in the sense of *count, compute, estimate, judge* when some basis of calculation or reckoning is stated or implied.

can, may   *Can* implies ability. *May* implies permission.

>   Can you swim?
>   Mother, may I go swimming?

cannot help but, can't help but   An idiom meaning "cannot fail to" or "to be compelled or obliged to." Purists object to its use in formal writing.

>   NOT: A good doctor cannot help but be interested in his patients.
>   BUT: A good doctor cannot help being interested in his patients.

capacity, ability   See **ability**.

case   One authority lists *case* as the greatest single source of jargon in technical writing. Although he might have difficulty proving his belief, the statement is helpful in emphasizing that some of the commonest and most objectionable examples of deadwood in writing occur in phrases employing *case*. The word accurately indicates a legal or medical problem. In other contexts, use it with discretion. The following phrases are frequently overused. When possible, choose a substitute.

>   in many cases (often, frequently)
>   in some cases (sometimes, occasionally)
>   in most cases (usually)
>   in case (if)
>   as is the case (as is true)
>   in each case (each time)

in other cases (sometimes)
such is the case (it is true)
in this case (here)
in the case of (for)
in any case (anyhow, anywhere)
in all cases (always)

Catchall words, like *case*, have their uses. In any case, see **Jargon.**

casual, causal Sometimes confused because of the similarity of spelling. *Casual* means "happening by chance," "coming without design or regularity," "occasional"; *causal* means "relating to a cause or expressing a cause."

A casual encounter often leads to lasting friendship.
The law of gravity defines a causal relation.

category Means "a division for the purpose of discussion or classification." It is often pretentiously and loosely used where *class* or *kind* would serve more accurately.

It is difficult to find men of that kind [*not* category].

caused by See **due to.**

center, middle These terms are not interchangeable. From its geometrical definition, *center* retains, even in nontechnical contexts, the idea of a point around which everything else revolves or rotates. *Middle* is less precise, suggesting a space rather than a point. Unlike *center, middle* does not necessarily suggest a circle and may be applied to what has duration (the middle of the day) or merely linear extension (the middle of the road).

the center of the ball, the middle of Ohio
The middle is the part that surrounds the center.

character Often used as jargon. Always carefully consider its usefulness in the sentence. The chances are that it will be deadwood. See **Jargon.**

NOT: Because of the erratic character of the lighting, the photographs were not usable.
BUT: Because of the erratic lighting, the photographs were not usable.
OR: The lighting was too erratic to furnish usable photographs.

claim Be careful when using this word in sentences like "You claim the watch stopped running." Such use often sounds accusing.

close proximity Since *proximity* means "the state of being near," omit the redundant word *close*. See **Redundancy.**

Colloquialism   A colloquial expression is one usually found in relaxed, familiar conversation rather than in formal writing. Applying this label to a word does not condemn it as illiterate. It means, rather, that if the tone of a letter or report is to be formal, a more formal synonym should be found for any word considered colloquial. Just as there is not 100 percent agreement on what makes an automobile classic or antique, so there is not 100 percent agreement about the status of many words labeled colloquial.

compare to, compare with   *Compare to* denotes general and figurative resemblance; *compare with* indicates specific similarities and differences.

> Love is compared to a rose in a famous poem.
> Please compare our annual report with theirs.

Compare to is useful when the things compared are essentially different but have some characteristic (often metaphorical) in common. Shakespeare asks, "Shall I compare thee to a summer's day?" because he thinks his lady "more lovely and more temperate" than a summer day and because the beauty of both is short-lived. To compare someone *with* a summer day would be ludicrous.

complected   Substandard. Use *complexioned.*

compose, comprise, include   Parts compose a whole; a whole comprises parts. Consequently, *compose* and *comprise* are analogous rather than synonymous, and *comprise* is roughly synonymous with *include.* However, *include* carries no suggestion that all parts have been named, whereas *comprise* definitely indicates that all parts are listed.

> Cement, aggregate, and water compose concrete.
> Concrete is composed of cement, aggregate, and water.
> Concrete comprises cement, aggregate, and water.
> Concrete includes cement and aggregate.

comprehensible, comprehensive   *Comprehensible* means "understandable"; *comprehensive* means "all-inclusive," "large in scope or content."

> A well-written report is comprehensible even to people without a technical background.
> A well-written report is comprehensive but concise.

comprise   See **compose.**

concept, conception Both words are overworked. Resist the urge to use them loosely for *idea, thought, notion, impression,* and so on.

conditions Often used superfluously.

> NOT: The tests were delayed by storm conditions.
> BUT: The tests were delayed by the storm.
> OR: The storm delayed the tests.

conduct *To conduct* means "to lead" or "to guide" and is roughly synonymous with *to manage, to control, to direct.* It always implies personal leadership or supervision. Don't use *conduct* loosely for *make, perform, accomplish, execute.*

> The director conducts the affairs of the bureau.
> The tests were performed.

confess See **admit.**

consensus of opinion Although some authorities accept it, this phrase is repetitive. *Consensus* means "an opinion held by all or most," "general agreement." See **Redundancy.**

> The consensus was that the program failed.

considerable Do not use for *considerably.*

considered opinion This phrase has become trite. In fact, *opinion,* which is stronger than *belief* and milder than *knowledge,* implies that the matter has been considered. Thus, *considered* should usually be omitted.

contact Widely used in America to mean "get in touch or communicate with," but objected to by purists. Try finding synonyms: *call, write, meet.*

contain, hold Don't use these words interchangeably. *Contain* connotes simply "to have within," whereas *hold* means "to have the capacity to contain or retain." Consequently, *contain* is used when the actual number, amount, or substance is indicated; *hold* is used when the capacity of the container is intended.

> The bottle, which holds a quart, contained only a pint.
> The box contains apples but holds five pounds.

contemptible, contemptuous *Contemptible* means "deserving contempt." *Contemptuous* means "feeling or expressing contempt."

> That was the most contemptible act I have ever witnessed.
> Everyone should be contemptuous of anyone who does that.

continual, continuous   *Continual* means "recurring frequently." *Continuous* means "without interruption."

> He is continually late for work.
> The horn blew continuously for an hour.

continuance, continuation, continuity   *Continuance* suggests lastingness first and an uninterrupted succession second. *Continuation* refers to the resumption after an interruption or to what continues as a supplement or installment. *Continuity* suggests unbrokenness primarily and extension secondarily.

> the continuance of an intelligent curiosity
> the continuation of a story
> the continuity of history

continue on   *On* is redundant. Say *continue.* See **Redundancy.**

Contractions   Some people think contractions are appropriate to speech but not to formal writing. Many writers use them freely to lighten tone when an air of intimacy or nonchalance is suitable to the context.

credible, credulous, creditable   *Credible* means "believable." *Credulous* means "willing to believe." *Creditable* means "praiseworthy."

data   A plural form. Its use as a singular form is gaining acceptance in the United States.

deal   Purists object when *deal* is used for *agreement, transaction.*

defective, deficient   Don't use these words interchangeably. *Defective* comes from *defect* and means "having imperfections, blemishes," etc. *Deficient* comes from *deficit* and means "lacking in completeness."

> Tests proved the gyroscope had a defective caging device.
> The test program was deficient because no runs were made in shark-infested waters.

definite, definitive   *Definite* means "clear," "unmistakable," "precise," "having fixed limits." *Definitive* means "unalterable," "final." That which is definitive is not subject to revision, debate, or alteration.

> A definite program is one in which the steps are clear.
> A definitive program is one that admits to no revision.
> Rayleigh's work on the measurement of sound intensity is definitive, but students often wish that his phrasing were more definite.

didn't ought See **had ought.**

different from, different than *Different from* is the preferred American form.

disinterested, uninterested *Disinterested* means "impartial." *Uninterested* means "indifferent," "having no pleasure or delight in something."

> A baseball umpire must be disinterested in the outcome of the game, but he should not be uninterested in the play.

distinct, distinctive *Distinct* means "set apart," "individual," "unlike others." *Distinctive* means "identifying characteristic."

> Each person has a distinct personality.
> The distinctive feature of this advertising campaign is that the manufacturer seems proud of the product's high price.

due consideration Trite and pretentious since it suggests that the writer knows how much consideration a subject deserves.

> NOT: After due consideration, I have abandoned the idea.
> BUT: After careful consideration, I have abandoned the idea.
> OR: I have considered the idea carefully and have abandoned it.

due to, because of, caused by, owing to Purists object to the use of *due to* as a preposition introducing an adverbial phrase:

> Due to an illness, he missed a lot of work.
> Due to a flood in early June, the entire tobacco crop was lost.

In both these examples, replacing *due to* with *because of* would eliminate the problem. *Owing to* is also acceptable in these sentences, but just why is hard to understand. Since *owing to* is not a comfortable idiom for most Americans, it is not likely to find great use in business writing anyway. There is no objection to the use of *due to* as an adjective:

> His absence was due to sickness.
> The tobacco crop loss was due to a flood in early June.

Perhaps the most graceful sentences could be composed if these troublesome phrases were avoided entirely.

> He was absent because he was sick.
> A flood in early June ruined the entire tobacco crop.

during the time that Substitute *while.*

effect See **affect.**

enthuse   *Enthuse* is colloquial for "to be enthusiastic" or "to be excited." Avoid it.

> NOT: He was enthused by the project.
> BUT: The project excited him.
> OR: He was enthusiastic about the project.

equable, equitable   What is *equable* is uniformly even or balanced, unvarying. What is *equitable* is fair, just, impartial.

> equable weather, an equable disposition
> an equitable trial, and equitable decision

equally as good   Redundant. Say "equally good" or "as good," but not both. See **Redundancy.**

> The product on the top shelf is as good as the one on the lower shelf.
> The product on the top shelf is equally good.

etc., et cetera   Means "and so forth." Don't use *etc.* as a substitute for specific items needed to extend a series. Don't use it to suggest that there are more in a series unless you know about other items not included. See also **and etc.**

evidence, proof   *Evidence* is an outward sign or indication of what may have happened. Enough evidence leads to *proof,* but evidence is not the same as proof. Evidence may be false or incomplete.

> NOT: As proof that two grams of vitamin C taken daily prevents colds, I offer the following clinical study.
> BUT: As evidence that two grams. . . .

except   See **accept.**

exceptional, exceptionable   These words are never interchangeable. *Exceptional* means "rare," "uncommon," "superior," "meritorious." *Exceptionable* means "liable to exception," hence "objectionable," "open to criticism."

> The Legion of Merit is given for exceptional service.
> Because of this exceptionable behavior the auditor was dismissed.

expect   Don't use *expect* as a synonym for *think* or *believe.*

> I think [*not* expect] the program is sound.
> I expect to go to Washington next week.

explicit, implicit   *Explicit* means "outspoken," "plainly stated," "having no hidden meaning," "clearly and apparently developed." *Implicit* means "implied," "understood though not expressed," "inherent though not shown."

Nowhere is it explicitly stated that the personnel manager must get approval to spend more than two hundred dollars.

Implicit in the regulations is the need to get the director's approval before spending any amount over two hundred dollars.

Do not use either *explicit* or *implicit* as a synonym for *complete, absolute,* or *full.*

I have complete [*not* explicit *or* implicit] faith in the accuracy of the report.

farther, further   Both can be used to indicate distance. *Further* also means "additional," "more." Also see **all the farther.**

I can't go any farther [*or* further].
I want to make one further point.

faze   Colloquial for *bother, disturb.*

NOT: It doesn't faze him.
BUT: It doesn't bother him.

feasible, possible   These two words, interchangeable in many contexts, have different shades of meaning. Both mean "capable of being realized." *Feasible* implies that a certain agency could bring about a certain event for a probable advantage. *Possible* implies that a thing may occur given the right conditions. *War is feasible* means that this may be a good time (for us) to go to war. *War is possible* means that conditions are such that war may break out.

It is feasible for scientists to create rainfall artificially.
It is possible that a thunderstorm will occur.

fellow   Colloquial for *person, boy, man.*

fewer, less   Use *fewer* for numbers. Use *less* for amounts or degrees. See **amount.**

There are fewer apples in this box than in that one.
There is less snow on the south slope than on the north.

few in number   Redundant. Omit *in number.* See **Redundancy.**

field   A catchall word used almost as extensively as *case,* often with no more justification. Refer to a field of a magnet, the field of an electric current, or a field of corn. Less definite meanings are frequently overworked and often redundant. See **Jargon.**

NOT: He excelled in the field of science.
BUT: He excelled in science.

finalize   Means "to make final," "to bring to completion." Purists object to this overused Americanism. Use a substitute or recast the sentence.

> NOT: Plans for the new County Home were finalized.
> BUT: Plans for the new County Home were completed.
> OR: We completed the plans for the new County Home.

final outcome   Needless repetition. Omit *final*. See **Redundancy.**

fine   Correctly used to mean "delicate," "excellently made," "sensitive," "subtle," "not coarse." Avoid as a term of general approval.

> The sales force had an excellent month in February.
> The manager does an excellent job in human relations.

first priority   Needless repetition. Omit *first*. See **Redundancy.**

fix   Colloquial for *predicament* ("The manager got himself into a fix") and *arrange* ("He fixed the election."). The word has many standard uses. One can fix the date of a ceremony, fix one's mind on a word, fix a color in cloth. It also has other colloquial and slang uses. Consult a dictionary.

foregone conclusion   Trite and meaningless. Avoid using it in the sense of *inevitable result* or *conclusion*.

further   See **farther.**

general rule   Illogical, since a rule that does not hold generally under the terms of its limitations is no rule at all. Either *as a rule* or *generally* is acceptable, but *usually* or *almost always* serves just as well.

get there, get to   Colloquial when used as substitutes for *arrive* or *arrive at.*

get through, get through to   Colloquial when used as a synonym for *finish, complete,* or *to communicate with.*

> I completed [*not* got through] the training program three days early.
> I tried to warn him of the danger, but I couldn't convince him [*not* get through to him].

get together   Colloquial for *assembled* or *organized.*

> The day shift assembled [*or* organized, *but not* got together] a softball team.

had better, had best, had rather   Acceptable forms.

> He had better hunt a new job soon.

had ought, didn't ought, hadn't ought Colloquial; redundant. Use *ought, should, should have, shouldn't have.*

hang, hung The principal parts of the verb are *hang, hung, hung,* but for capital punishment they are *hang, hanged, hanged.* You hang people and people are hanged. You hang objects and objects are hung. People are not hung; they are hanged. Pictures are not hanged; they are hung.

hardly, scarcely *Hardly* and *scarcely* are negatives. Don't use them with another negative.

> NOT: He knows hardly nothing about the job.
> BUT: He knows hardly anything about the job.
>
> NOT: Without scarcely a hesitation, he fired the group leader.
> BUT: With scarcely a hesitation, he fired the group leader.

healthful, healthy *Healthful* means "promoting health." *Healthy* means "having health."

> Fresh air is healthful.
> The child is healthy.

hold See **contain.**

hopefully Widely misused instead of *I hope, one hopes, it is hoped,* as in "This year, hopefully, will be more profitable for the company than last year." Writers who use the term this way intend an ellipsis, that is, an omission of words necessary for complete grammatical construction but understood by the context of the sentence: "This year, and I say this hopefully, will be more profitable for the company than last year." It is better to break the habit than to defend it.

> NOT: Careful writers will, hopefully, abandon it.
> BUT: Careful writers will, I hope, abandon it.

idea A catchall word that pops into a weary writer's mind before the word he really needs can suggest itself. Try to find a precise term. See **Jargon.**

> NOT: My idea is to buy a mobile home park.
> BUT: My plan [*or* intention] is to buy a mobile home park.

if, whether Both are acceptable, but purists prefer *whether or not.*

> I don't know if [*or* whether] I should go.
> I don't know whether or not I should go.

implicit　See **explicit.**

imply, infer　*Imply* means "to hint," "to suggest," "to indicate indirectly." *Infer* means "to come to a conclusion," "to derive by reasoning."

> The personnel manager implied that he would recommend me for the job.
> From his remarks, I infer that he will recommend me.

important essentials　Redundant. Anything essential has to be important. See **Redundancy.**

in back of　See **back of.**

include　See **compose.**

incredible, incredulous　*Incredible* means "not believable." *Incredulous* means "not able to believe." Statements or assertions are incredible. People are incredulous.

individual　Don't use *individual* carelessly as a synonym for *person.*

> NOT: He is a gifted individual.
> BUT: He is a gifted person.

infer　See **imply.**

ingenious, ingenuous　*Ingenious* means "gifted with genius," "possessed with ingenuity," "clever," "adroit," "shrewd." *Ingenuous* means "free from restraint or disguise," "without guile," "simple," "artless," "candid," "naive."

> His on-the-spot modification was ingenious.
> His ingenuous manner was carefully cultivated as an aid in selling gold bricks.

in nature　See **nature.**

in regards to　Substandard. Use *regarding* or *in regard to.*

inside of　*Of* in the expression *inside of* is redundant. Omit it. See **Redundancy.** Do not use *inside of* for *within.*

> The gauge was installed inside [*not* inside of] the chamber.
> Give me the report within [*not* inside of] one week.

invaluable　See **valuable.**

irregardless　Substandard. Use *regardless.*

is because　*Because* introduces an adverbial clause of reason. It cannot logically follow the linking verb *to be*. Substitute *that* for *because*.

> The reason he lost his job is that [*not* because] he alienated the chief of purchasing.

Better yet, avoid the problem by recasting the sentence.

> He lost his job because he alienated the chief of purchasing.

Also see **reason is because.**

is when, is where   Avoid these constructions.

> NOT: Arson is when a house is set afire.
> BUT: Intentionally burning a house is arson.
> NOT: Pittsburgh is where the Allegheny and the Monongahela rivers meet to form the Ohio.
> BUT: The Allegheny and the Monongahela rivers meet in Pittsburgh to form the Ohio.

it, there   Sentences beginning with *it* or *there* are often wordy.

> NOT: It is the belief of many administrators that. . . .
> BUT: Many administrators believe that. . . .
>
> NOT: There are some who think that. . . .
> BUT: Some people think. . . .

its, it's   *Its* is the possessive form of *it*. *It's* is a contraction of *it is*. Because it indicates possession with nouns, the apostrophe sometimes is mistakenly used with the possessive form.

Jargon   A derogatory term applied to incomprehensible language, usually the specialized language of a trade or profession. Jargon is often filled with catchall words like *aspect, case, factor, field, important, nice, point,* and *thing*. The writer who uses it is usually more interested in impressing the reader than in being clear. Jargon is very useful when writing for colleagues who will know what you mean with the scantest of clues. It is also useful when you have something to say but can't decide exactly what it is. Jargon is absolutely essential when you want to hide the fact that there is little meaning in the passage. Keep jargon out of your writing and be suspicious when you see it. See section 30, "How to Choose the Right Word," under *Catchall Words*.

kind of, sort of   Colloquial when used before an adjective in the sense of *rather*.

> Her methods were rather [*not* kind of] haphazard.

know-how   Substandard for *knowledge* and *experience*.

lay, lie　*Lay* means "to put" or "to place." *Lay, laid, laid* are the principal parts.

> I laid the file on the second shelf in February.
> I would have laid it there sooner, but I had to use it.
> I should go over there and lay it on the first shelf.

Lie means "to recline." *Lie, lay, lain* are the principal parts.

> Right now the file lies on the second shelf.
> It lay there yesterday and the day before that.
> In fact, it has lain there for two months.
> It has been lying on the second shelf too long.

leave, let　*Leave* means "to depart from" or "allow to remain." *Let* means "to allow" or "permit."

> Leave the room right now and leave the book on the table before you go.
> Do not let anyone leave the building without a card.
> Don't let anyone destroy your confidence.

lend　See **loan.**

let　See **leave.**

liable, likely　*Liable* means "the probability of an unfavorable or unpleasant result." *Likely* refers to a probability of any kind.

> Speeding makes one liable to arrest.
> If one speeds consistently, he is likely to be arrested.
> If you buy enough tickets, you are likely [*not* liable] to win.

lie　See **lay.**

like　Don't use *like* as a conjunction unless you are trying for a special effect.

> FAULTY: Avoid smoking cigarettes like the surgeon general says you should.
> CORRECT: Avoid smoking cigarettes as the surgeon general recommends.

likely　See **liable.**

line　Jargon for *profession* or *trade,* as in "What line of work are you in?" See **Jargon.**

loan, lend　Both are now used as verbs meaning "to let someone have something for a period of time with the expectation that he will return it, usually with interest." Purists prefer to use *loan* as a noun and *lend* as a verb.

locate Don't use as a synonym for "move to," "take up residence," "settle."

> Germans settled [*not* located] in Pennsylvania.

lot, lots Avoid as synonyms for *much* and *many*.

> NOT: Lots of employees prefer a winter vacation.
> BUT: Many employees prefer a winter vacation.

materialize A pretentious substitute for *appear* or *happen*.

> Difficulties with the training program appeared [*not* materialized] early.

matter Another catchall word often vaguely used. Hunt the exact word needed by the context. See **Jargon.**

> Investigate the complaint [*not* matter] at once.
> Please give this request [*not* matter] your immediate attention.

may See **can.**

most Not a substitute for *almost*.

> Almost all [*not* most all] the tractors sold that month had faulty tires.

myself Don't use *myself* out of a sense of modesty to avoid saying *I* or *me*.

> After you have filled out the form, return it to either my secretary or me [*not* myself].

You may properly use *myself* for emphasis, as in "I myself will hold the target."

nature, in nature Omit these terms when they are unnecessary for the intended meaning.

> NOT: Because of the fluid nature of the medium, ...
> BUT: Because the medium is fluid, ...
> NOT: Since dandelion is bitter in nature, it may be more palatable cooked.
> BUT: Since dandelion is bitter, it may be more palatable cooked.

noted, notorious People famous in a desirable way are *noted*. People with unsavory reputations are *notorious*.

nothing like, nothing near, nowhere near Colloquialisms. Use *not nearly*.

nowheres See **anywheres.**

of Don't use in place of *have* in *should have, would have, might have*.

off of   *Of* in this phrase can often be omitted.

> We threw the cartons off the truck.

of the fact, of the fact that   Try to omit these usually redundant phrases from your sentences. See **Redundancy.**

> NOT: He was aware of the fact that the contract had been lost.
> BUT: He was aware that the contract had been lost.
>
> NOT: Because of the fact that the clearance had not arrived, ...
> BUT: Because the clearance had not arrived, ...

on the part of   A vague, wordy, and awkward phrase better cut from most sentences.

> NOT: Full cooperation on the part of the Advertising Department will guarantee success of the project.
> BUT: If the Advertising Department cooperates, the project will succeed.

owing to   See **due to.**

per   Avoid when possible. Also see **as per.**

> NOT: ten cents per yard
> BUT: ten cents a yard

Although *per diem, per annum, per se* are in good standing, use English equivalents when possible.

phase   Another catchall word you should scrutinize before keeping in a sentence. See **Jargon.**

plan on   Colloquial. Use *plan to.*

> NOT: plan on going
> BUT: plan to go

point   An overworked catchall word. See **Jargon.**

possible   See **feasible.**

posted   Colloquial when used for *informed.* Keep this use of *posted* out of formal contexts.

> The division chief will keep us informed [*not* posted].

practical, practicable   Not strictly synonymous. *Practical* "stresses effectiveness as tested by actual experience or as measured by a completely realistic approach to life or the particular circumstances involved." *Practicable* "is used of something that appears to be capable of being put into effect, but has not yet been developed or tried." (These definitions are from *Webster's New World Dictionary,* 2d college ed.)

Many once thought that an internal combustion engine was not practicable, but now it is one of our most practical instruments.

previous to, prior to   Usually used as long and cumbersome substitutes for *before*.

principal, principle   The one that ends in *pal* is the chief. A principal is the chief of a school. The chief reason is the principal reason.

prior to   See **previous to.**

proof   See **evidence.**

providing   Don't use *providing* in sentences where *if* will serve as well or better.

> I will pay the fee if [*not* providing] you agree to service the equipment for six months.

purposes   Thoughtlessly used, this word often serves for padding without adding to meaning. See **Jargon.**

> NOT: The instrument was used for test purposes.
> BUT: The instrument was used for testing.

put across, put over, put it up to, put in   Many of these idioms of *put* are trite, slangy, or otherwise objectionable.

> NOT: We put over our plan.
> BUT: Our plan was approved.
>
> NOT: The question was put up to the boss.
> BUT: We let the boss decide.

re   Meaning "concerning," "referring to," *re* is overworked in many business contexts.

react, reaction   Don't use loosely for *feel, think, respond* or for *effect, influence, opinion, feeling, impression.*

> NOT: What was the manager's reaction to the proposal?
> BUT: Did the manager approve the proposal?

real   Avoid using *real* as a substitute for *very* or *really*.

> The supervisor was very [*or* really *but not* real] upset.

reason is because   A sentence beginning "The reason is . . . ." requires for completion either an adjective or a noun. It cannot be correctly completed by an adverb. Usually, the best construction is a noun clause introduced by *that*. See **is because.**

> The reason we have no left-handed second basemen is that [*not* because] a left-hander could not throw easily to first base.

reason why *Why* is redundant in *the reason why* construction. Omit *why*. Notice, too, that many sentences using the word *reason* are wordy and should be recast.

> REDUNDANT: The reason why we have so few customers is that our location is inconvenient.
>
> WORDY: The reason we have so few customers is that our location is inconvenient.
>
> BETTER: Our inconvenient location is keeping away customers.

reckon See **calculate.**

Redundancy Needless repetition in a construction is called a redundancy. "Advance to the front," "continue on," "left-handed southpaw" are obvious examples.

respectfully, respectively *Respectfully* means "with respect," "showing or intending respect," "in a respectful manner." *Respectively* means "in the order indicated," or "in a certain specified order."

> The umpire asked Smith, Jones, and Harmon to go back to first, second, and third bases respectively.
>
> He might have said it respectfully, but that's doubtful.

same Don't use *same* as a pronoun.

> We collected the letters and mailed them [*not* same].

sanguine, sanguinary *Sanguine* means "cheerful," "optimistic." *Sanguinary* means "bloody."

scarcely See **hardly.**

shall, will For most business and technical writing contexts you can forget about the old admonition to use *shall* with the first person and *will* with the others. *Will* has almost completely replaced *shall*, except in expressions like "What shall we do now?" Although many purists prefer to retain the distinction, *will* is correct in general usage.

> We will be interviewing in Baltimore next week.
> I will be very happy to recommend you.
> I will go no matter what you say.

Even in the last example with the emphasis on *will* to show determination, *will* is commonly used instead of *shall*.

should, would Like *will*, *would* is now commonly and correctly used with the first person. The use of *should* often implies an obligation or an act of prudence.

I should write to my partner.

We should transfer our insurance account.

Would indicates a willingness to do something under certain conditions.

I would buy from them if their salesmen were not so surly.

Would also expresses a customary action done in the past, synonymous with *used to.*

Every Monday afternoon he would fall asleep in the operations committee meeting.

somewheres   See **anywheres.**

sort of   See **kind of.**

stationary, stationery   *Stationary* means "fixed in place." The one with *er* stands for pap*er*—writing paper, that is.

take   See **bring.**

that, which   Both are used as relative pronouns. *That* refers to either persons or things; *which,* only to things. A distinction some people make is to use *that* to introduce restrictive clauses and *which* to introduce nonrestrictive clauses.

The *Great Eastern* is the ship that was used to lay the Atlantic cable. [*restrictive*]

The *Great Eastern,* which was the largest ship of its day, was used to lay the Atlantic cable. [*nonrestrictive*]

However, *which* is widely used to introduce restrictive clauses.

The ship which was used to lay the Atlantic cable was the *Great Eastern.*

there   See **it.**

thing   Another catchall word, often used without a precise meaning. See **Jargon.**

NOT: The first thing to do is remove the ribbon.

BUT: First, remove the ribbon.

this   Be wary of using *this* to refer to an entire idea expressed in a preceding sentence rather than to a definite noun. The result is usually unclear and confusing.

VAGUE: The supervisor said that henceforth the maintenance crew would go directly from lunch to the locker room. This provoked a great deal of resentment from the workers.

IMPROVED: This change in policy [*or* this announcement] provoked. . . .

If *this* is used to refer generally to an idea, the reference must be perfectly clear.

> The new industry has increased the standard of living in the area about 200 percent. This has been a very welcome improvement.

together   See **assemble together.**

too numerous to mention   Trite, affected, and sometimes insulting. It is put at the end of a short list to indicate that there are many more. It usually means that the writer believes there are more but can't remember what they are.

total effect of all this   Wordy. Just say *the effect.*

true facts   Like *the honest truth*, *true facts* is needlessly repetitive. Say *the truth* and *the facts.* See **Redundancy.**

uninterested   See **disinterested.**

unique   Means "only one of its kind." Something can't be more unique than something else. *Unique* is not synonymous with *rare* or *strange.* Other adjectives that cannot be compared are *round* and *perfect.* The writers of the Preamble to the Constitution forgot this rule: "In order to form a more perfect union. . . ." It happens to the best people.

valuable, invaluable   Don't use *invaluable* when you mean only *valuable. Invaluable* means "having value beyond measure."

where   Don't use *where* as a substitute for *that.* Also see **is when.**

> I read that [*not* where] Alpha is going to merge with Beta.

whether, whether or not   See **if.**

which   See **that.**

who, whom; whoever, whomever   The movement to throw *whom* and *whomever* out of the English language will probably succeed in a hundred years. If you are not sure you can wait that long, here is a way to pick the right form when writing. Substitute *he* and *him* in the slot where *who* or *whom* will go. If *he* works, you want *who;* if *him* works, you want *whom.* For example, if your sentence is

> I gave some money to a person (who, whom) I trust.

recast and substitute:

> I gave some money to a person. I trust (he, him).

Him works, so you know you need *whom*.

> I gave some money to a person whom I trust.

Try it again.

> I gave some money to a broker (who, whom), I trust, will turn a profit for me.

Now, substitute:

> I gave some money to a broker. I trust (he, him) will turn a profit for me.

He works, so you know you must use *who*.

> I gave some money to a broker who, I trust, will turn a profit for me.

will   See **shall.**

-wise   A suffix attached to a noun to make an adverb. Recast your sentence to avoid this substandard form.

> NOT: Experience-wise, he's not qualified for the job.
> BUT: He doesn't have enough experience for the job.
> OR: He doesn't have the proper experience for the job.

would   See **should.**

write-up   Colloquial for *report, memo,* or *written account.*

> NOT: Get me the write-up on automated chicken feeders.
> BUT: Get me the report [*or* memo *or* brochure] on automated chicken feeders.

your   Not a substitute for *a, an,* or *the* when there is no possession. Use *your* only to indicate possession.

> NOT: He's not your ordinary thief.
> BUT: He's not an ordinary thief.

SECTION 32

How to Punctuate

To understand the importance of punctuation, look at a piece of writing without any:

> There is no single system for good bar spacing the reason for this is that several things have an effect on how thick the bars seem the size and shape of the chart the number of bars the length of the bars and even the

shading used in them for example bars that are the right thickness in a chart 4 inches wide would be too long and thin in a chart 8 inches wide satisfactory bars can be designed however by following this basic principle the shorter or closer the bars the thinner they should be the longer or farther apart the bars the thicker they should be

The passage was chosen at random and does not represent any special problem. Nevertheless, you can see that reading much material without punctuation, while possible, would be bothersome. Probably 90 percent of the time punctuation is just a gentle aid to clarity, but the other 10 percent of the time it is crucial to meaning. Be careful not to overlook any of these times in the messages you write. The more carefully phrased the passage, the less punctuation contributes to clarity. Never ask punctuation to rescue a bad construction. Rephrase it.

Punctuation aids clarity by suggesting some of the characteristics of the spoken language—the pitch, intonation, pause, and stress the speaker employs. In earlier times, when it was expected that written material would be rendered once again in speech, writers punctuated lavishly. Today's speed readers want only the necessary marks.

Skillful punctuation approaches art. Use it and think of it along with all the other techniques you know, such as capitalization and use of white space, for communicating your meaning. Learn the possible uses of each mark, and select the one that does the job best.

The Period

1. Use a period, with two typing spaces following, to end a declarative sentence.

   The airlines are moving into a period of uncertain costs.

2. Use a period to end an imperative sentence.

   Sweep the floor and lock the desks.

3. Use a period at the end of a polite request phrased like a question.

   Will you please close the door when you leave.

4. Use a period after the initials of a name.

   R. D. Timm

   One space follows the period after an initial. However, in annotations to a letter no period or space follows.

   NOL:RD

5. Use a period after most abbreviations.

    Ariz.   Ave.   Cwt.   Mfg.

6. Use three spaced periods (. . .), or ellipsis points, to show that you are omitting words from a quotation.

    "Thanks largely to the efficiency of jets . . . airlines grew accustomed to traffic growth each year."

    Use a sentence period plus ellipsis points if the omission comes at the end of the sentence.

    "Job training and job development are the daily concern of profit-making enterprises. . . ."

7. Use a period for the decimal point in figures. No typing space follows.

    8.61 tons $6.98

8. Use a period after the identifying elements of an outline.

    I.
        A.
        B.
            1.
            2.
                a.
                b.

9. Don't use periods after roman numbers in a sentence.

    In spite of his World War II injuries, he was one of our most skillful crane operators.

    However, avoid using roman numbers whenever possible; arabic numbers are simpler; *23*, for example, is almost always better than *XXIII*.

10. Don't use a period after a letter used to identify an object or to indicate a fictitious person.

    File A is still incomplete.
    Mr. X called again tonight.

11. Don't use a period after *percent*.

    All loading dock employees will get a 2 percent raise this year.

    Note that figures, not spelled-out words, are generally used before the word *percent*.

12. Don't use periods after chemical symbols.

    H_2O NaCl

The Question Mark

1. Use a question mark, with two typing spaces following, at the end of a direct question.

   How can profits be too high?

2. Use a question mark at the end of a sentence that asks a question even if the form is declarative.

   Profits are too high?

3. Some sentences are part question, part statement. Use the end punctuation suggested by the final clause.

   The Federal Energy Office has never considered the use to be excessive, but even if it had, would there be any recourse?

   Why shouldn't it—although I do realize the problem.

4. A question mark is sometimes used to indicate doubt about the accuracy of a statement.

   The Hager Company is 40 (?) years old.

5. Note the placement of a question mark in relationship to quotation marks. Always put periods inside quotation marks, but try to follow logic with question marks. (Sometimes, as in the first example, circumstances make it impossible.) There is no space between a question mark and the closing quote.

   Do you think a house organ should run a story called "Who Killed Private Enterprise?"

   Isn't that an example of what William Vaughan Moody might call "a dull commercial liturgy"?

   Today's *Wall Street Journal* carries an article entitled "Do We Need a Nuclear Test Ban?"

The Exclamation Point

1. Use an exclamation point with two typing spaces following, at the end of a sentence expressing strong feeling. The form of the sentence could suggest a simple statement, a command, or even a question.

   I will never sell that house!
   Call the police!
   What kind of salesman would do a thing like that!

The same sentences convey another kind of meaning when ended with punctuation showing less emotion.

I will never sell that house.

Call the police. [*No need to be excited, but the police should be notified.*]

What kind of salesman would do a thing like that? [*Here more curiosity than indignation is suggested.*]

2. Do not space between an exclamation point and the closing quote.

He turned, looked at each of us, and said, "Idiots!"

3. If you use an exclamation point after an emphatic remark, the next word should be capitalized.

Outstanding! Send letters of praise to each member.

4. Use exclamation marks sparingly; overuse diminishes effectiveness.

Quotation Marks

1. Titles of books, plays, musical and other artistic works are usually indicated by italics (underlining), but quotation marks are also acceptable.

2. A word used as a word may be either italicized or enclosed in quotation marks.

Some people salivate when they hear the word "lemon."

3. Use quotes to indicate slang in formal writing. You may use quotes judiciously to flag unfamiliar technical words or other special uses of words. Use this device only in special circumstances. Don't overuse.

4. Use single quotes to indicate a quotation within a quotation.

"He said it to me again just last night," she said, fighting back the tears. " 'I will never leave this office; they will carry me out feet first.' I can still hear his voice."

5. If quoted material goes to several paragraphs, put quotes at the beginning of each paragraph and at the end of the entire quotation.

6. Use quotation marks to indicate what was said. Don't use quotation marks with indirect quotations.

"I will never leave this office," he said.

He told her that he would never leave the office.

7. Punctuation accompanying a quotation varies.

> He said "baloney" and kept on walking. [*None in short quoted remarks.*]
>
> The chairman said without hesitation, "We didn't come here to exchange insults." [*A comma after a short introduction to a short quotation.*]
>
> The speaker approached the lectern with a malicious glint in his eye. Then he delivered his thesis: "The New Yorker is an interesting breed, with enough gall to be divided into three parts. He asks the rest of the world to send their finest goods to him. And in return he offers to tell them how to run their lives." [*A colon after a formal introduction to a long passage.*]

Note other conventions for punctuating quotations.

> "I would work here anyway," Harold said.
> "Even if they didn't pay you?" Mildred said incredulously.
> "I owe them my very life," Harold replied.
> Mildred shook her head sadly. "That's exactly how they want you to feel."
> "Ridicule it if you like," he said evenly, "but my mind is made up."

Always put periods and commas inside closing quotes. Always put colons and semicolons outside closing quotes. Put dashes, question marks, exclamation points, and closing parentheses inside closing quotes when they pertain to the quoted material only. Put them outside the closing quote when they pertain to the whole sentence.

8. Short quotations are enclosed in quotation marks and are run right in the normal text. Long quotations are indented and single-spaced and need not be enclosed in quotation marks so long as the text itself indicates the quotation and gives credit. See section 28, "How to Use Other People's Writing," for examples and exceptions.

The Comma

1. Items in a series—words, phrases, clauses, figures, signs—should be separated by commas. Use a comma before the conjunction that connects the last item in the series.

> The language of the memo is something less than sharp, clear, and precise.
>
> George rolled up his sleeves, took a deep breath, and started to work.
>
> I believe that she is well qualified, that she has earned a promotion, and that she is the best person for the job.
>
> Please refer to items A, B, C, and D in the contract.

2. Use a comma between adjectives of equal rank. Don't use a comma if they are not of equal rank. One way to test is to supply an *and*. If it fits, use a comma.

> A tall, dark, handsome man stood in the doorway.
> He wore a light brown suit.

3. Use a comma before the conjunction in a compound sentence, except when the sentence is very short.

> Everybody knows that it's a problem, but nobody knows what to do about it.
> I looked at the record and he understood.

4. Use a comma to show the omission of a verb in the second part of a compound sentence.

> Mr. Eckenroad runs a shoe store; his wife, a beauty shop.

5. Use a comma after an introductory clause or phrase.

> Although the project was long overdue, certain aspects of it are causing problems.
> If the government monitors the cutbacks, the plan may work.

Other words introducing such clauses are *while, because, whereas, as,* and others. Short clauses are sometimes not set off by commas if there is no chance that they will be misread.

> After the horn sounded they went home.

6. Don't put a comma between a noun clause and the verb.

> What the citizens fear most is a major depression.

7. Use good judgment in punctuating introductory elements. If the introductory part is long, or there is some ambiguity, punctuate or recast the sentence. When the dependent clause follows the main clause, you may use a comma if you consider the dependent clause to carry an additional meaning not necessary to the intent of the main clause. Otherwise no comma should be used.

> Brazil has not abandoned coffee, if that is a comfort to anybody.
> Newton Manufacturing has given up advertising because their product sells without it.
> Mr. Weedon will probably make the announcement when the ship comes into port.

8. Use commas to set off other nonrestrictive (not needed for the meaning of the sentence) clauses.

> Robert R. Robbins, who is executive vice president of Purex, attributed the poor performance of its subsidiary to a bad labor situation.

9. Do not use commas if a clause is needed for a complete understanding of the sentence.

> The file that contained the forged document was turned over to the FBI.

10. Use commas to set off appositives of more than one word.

> S. S. Pierce, a food firm based in Boston, planted more than 2,000 acres of strawberries in blocks as big as 500 acres.

11. Use commas to set off parenthetical and transitional expressions, such as *accordingly, in the first place, however, nevertheless, moreover, indeed, of course, consequently.*

> However, the penalty is too great to make the risk acceptable.

Note, however, that *however* may not call for commas.

> However great the risk, we must not falter.

12. Use a comma after *yes* or *no* at the beginning of a sentence answering a question.

> Yes, flight 897 was on time.

13. Use a comma before *such as* when it introduces a short series. Don't use the comma if *such* and *as* are separated by a noun.

> Articles of guerilla warfare, such as grenades, rifles, molotov cocktails, were found in the locker.

> The locker contained such articles as grenades, rifles, and molotov cocktails.

14. Use a comma after such expressions as *for example, that is, i.e., namely.*

> Some analysts have been put off by the agency's accounting system, that is, amortizing advertising costs over a 36-month period.

15. Use a comma to set off the name of a person addressed.

> We are very sorry, Mrs. Wray, that you had an unfortunate experience with our pancake mix.

16. Use a comma between the day of the week and the month and between the day of the month and the year. Use a comma after the year if the sentence continues.

> Classes begin Thursday, March 10, 1977, in the classroom now assigned to the engineering division.

You can join the growing trend to simplify by putting the day of the month in front of the name of the month and to use no commas at all.

> 10 March 1977

17. Use a comma between the name of the city and the name of the state and between the name of the state and the rest of the sentence. Note, too, that the comma is usually omitted between the name of the month and the year.

    The club was built in Big Hollow, Iowa, in June 1921.

18. Use a comma after the complimentary close of a letter.

    Very truly yours,   Sincerely yours,

19. In alphabetical arrangements of names and titles, commas are used as follows:

    Carvell, Fred J.   *Human Relations in Business*
    Cavanagh, G. F.   *Businessperson in Search of Values, The*

20. Use a comma between a name and a title that follows it.

    Mr. Albright Krome, Jr.
    Mr. Fearless K. Leader, Manager
    Miss Joan Dark, Ph.D.

21. Use a comma where needed to prevent misreading.

    Two hours after they ate, the dog ran away.
    Instead of hundreds, thousands came.
    To Henry, Maxwell seemed dishonest.

22. Use a comma to set off introductory modifiers from the noun modified.

    Surrounded by enemies, they surrendered.
    Weary but cheerful, Valerie left the office.
    Of all firms surveyed, the most efficient is Company Z.

23. Use a comma after a question followed by a question.

    You will go, won't you?
    But you voted for the bill, didn't you?

24. Use a comma between the title of a person and the name of the organization when *of* or *of the* is omitted.

    Deputy Head, Department of Transportation
    Chief, Finance Division

25. Use a comma to identify thousands, millions, and so on, in numbers of more than three digits.

    9,300   48,899   50,000,000

    In financial writing it is common to omit the commas in four-digit sums of money.

    $2531

Don't use commas in built-up fractions, decimals, and serial numbers, telephone numbers, street numbers, etc.

motor number 234567890	1.6084
Social Security number 193–14–9880	1/2500
army serial number 13090413	page 1162
2345 Bush Street	Executive Order 44567

26. Don't use a comma before the ampersand in the name of a company.

    Hart, Shaffner & Marx

27. Commas are always placed inside closing quotes. See *Quotation Marks*, this section.

28. The trend today is not to use commas where there is no significant pause. When in doubt you may leave them out unless misreading results.

The Semicolon

1. The semicolon functions as a weak period or as a strong comma. In general, avoid its use anywhere that a period would be acceptable. Use it instead of a comma in any circumstance where a comma would not make an adequate separation.

2. Use a semicolon instead of a period if two sentences are closely related in thought.

    He made money on the bananas; he lost money on the oranges.

    Another way of saying the same thing is that a semicolon may be used in a compound sentence when the conjunction and the comma are not used.

3. Two thoughts joined by adverbs like *moreover, consequently, also, therefore, hence, meanwhile,* and *yet* are usually separated by a semicolon (sometimes by a period). If you want to emphasize the adverb, put a comma after it.

    He had a great opportunity to speak to the ordinary man on the street; however, he seemed more interested in impressing the educated.

    He must have felt the intellectuals were more important; otherwise he would have used the common touch.

4. You may use a semicolon to separate the clauses of a compound sentence if either or both of the clauses contain commas.

> He had no intention of catering to crooks, thugs, and derelicts; but he was frequently seen in dark, smelly alleys where decent people feared to go.

5. Use semicolons to separate items in a series if members of the series contain commas.

> The old trunk contained two rifles, a Winchester and a Savage; three boxes of bullets, caliber 32 and 30-30; assorted bolts, some with nuts screwed on and some without; a box of pocket watches, one Hamilton, one Elgin, and several old railroad watches, the kind that wind with a key; a Civil War scarf, faded and stained, with what looked like a bullet hole at the place where it would cross the throat.

6. You may use a semicolon before *for example, e.g., that is, namely, viz.,* and *for instance* when they introduce a list or series. Use a comma after these words.

> Only durable goods should be included; for example, stoves, refrigerators, washing machines.

The Colon

1. The colon is a mark used to suggest that something follows: what follows may be an explanation, a list, or an example implied in the statement that precedes the colon:

> The accord raises a number of questions. Among them: Do the belligerents want and need a full-scale peace?
>
> My friend did a very foolish thing: she got married.
>
> Recommendation: Answer all letters the day they are received.
>
> We will be glad to send you the books you ordered: *The Hex Sign, The Sign of the Hex, Hexerei.*
>
> And then he launched into this rendition of "The Face on the Barroom Floor":

Some writers are able to avoid the colon. You can read long passages without seeing one. Yet if you study its uses, you will find it a handy mark.

2. In a letter use a colon after the salutation and to separate the initials of the dictator and stenographer.

> Dear Mr. Fitz: RSF:DG

3. Use a colon to separate place of publication and publishing company in bibliographic entries.

>   Pennsburg: Industrial Historians, Inc.

4. Use a colon when stating clock time.

>   2:30

5. Use a colon when citing a biblical reference.

>   Genesis 4:3

The Apostrophe

1. If a singular noun does not end in s, form its possessive by adding 's.

>   child, child's   man, man's

2. If a singular noun does end in s, or in an s sound, you may form its possessive by adding an apostrophe only or by adding 's.

>   boss, boss' *or* boss's
>   waitress, waitress' *or* waitress's

Because—regardless of spelling—the s sound is pronounced, many writers prefer to form all singular possessives by adding 's.

3. Plural nouns are easier. Most of them do end in s. Form their possessives by adding an apostrophe only.

>   directors, directors'   clerks, clerks'

If a plural noun does not end in s, form its possessive by adding 's.

>   children, children's   men, men's

4. Form possessives of proper names just like other nouns.

>   Howard, Howard's
>   Gladys, Gladys' *or* Gladys's
>   John Jones, John Jones' *or* John Jones's
>   the Joneses, the Joneses'

5. For compound nouns, add 's to the word nearest the thing possessed.

>   the inspector general's report
>
>   The man with the flowing white beard's hat. [*Technically correct as far as placing the possessive is concerned, but, clearly, the sentence should be recast.*]

6. Show joint possession by adding 's to the last word of a pair or a series. If you want to show individual possession, you must place an apostrophe after each.

> men and women's lounge [*one lounge shared*]
> men's and women's lounges [*two lounges*]
> Kennedy and Johnson's administration
> Kennedy's, Johnson's, and Nixon's administrations

7. For names of organizations, firm names, geographic names, use the form adopted by the entity involved.

> Johns Hopkins University
> Harpers Ferry
> St. Peter's Cathedral

8. Where the form suggests possession but the intention is more descriptive, don't use an apostrophe.

> editors handbook   teachers college   Teamsters Union

But when the plural does not end in s, an apostrophe is needed to avoid the appearance of a spelling error.

> Children's Hospital   Young Men's Christian Association

9. Remember: Possessive pronouns do not take an apostrophe.

> yours   hers   his   its   ours   theirs

Other pronouns in the possessive case take 's.

> one's opinion   somebody's dog   each other's arms

10. Where number is not clearly understood, choose the singular possessive form.

> cow's milk   printer's ink   traveler's checks

11. Sometimes a possessive form is used even though there is no ownership.

> two weeks' notice   for pity's sake

If a word ends in s or an s sound and is followed by a word beginning in s, add only an apostrophe, in order to avoid a disagreeable sound.

> for goodness' sake   for conscience' sake

12. Remember: A noun before a gerund should be in the possessive case.

> He was annoyed by the boy's coughing.
> In the event of the stock's falling in price. . . .

13. Apostrophes help to show two other tricky forms of possession.

> Danks' [Danks' store] is having a sale.
>
> Harrigan is a friend of mine.
> Harrigan is a friend of Bill's [not of Bill].

14. Don't use apostrophes in abbreviations.

> Sgt.　　　pvt.　　　coon　　　copter
> asst.　　　Ltd.　　　possum　　Atty. Gen.

15. Use an apostrophe to show contractions, the omission of a letter or figure, and to show the plurals of letters, figures, and abbreviations.

> it's, doesn't, we'll, ma'am
> p's and q's, the three R's
> class of '43, the 49'ers
> Btu.'s, dept.'s

16. Don't use apostrophes to show plurals of spelled-out numbers or words used as words.

> Everything is at sixes and sevens.
> There are no ifs, ands, or buts about it.

But use 's if omission would make reading difficult.

> Here is a list of do's and don'ts.
> Your report has too many which's and that's.

The Hyphen

1. Make the hyphen with one stroke of the hyphen key on the typewriter. Do not space before or after the mark.

2. Use a hyphen to show that a word divided at the end of a line continues on the next. When you need to divide a word, consult your dictionary and refer to section 34, "How to Break Words."

3. In business writing, words and word elements are constantly being combined to form word clusters and new words. At first, hyphens separate the elements. As use makes a combination familiar, the hyphens disappear. The combination has a good chance of becoming a closed compound if the total number of syllables is under five:

> air line　　　air-line　　　airline
> none the less　none-the-less　nonetheless

If the number of syllables is over five, the hyphens usually drop out, leaving a collection of individual words:

color-television set   color television set

The combination you are thinking of hyphenating may not be in the dictionary. Then what do you do? Try to recast the sentence to avoid the problem.

NOT: This is a decision-making group.
BUT: This group makes decisions.

NOT: This is an echelon-above-division decision.
BUT: Some echelon higher than division must make this decision.

In the latter example, the recast sentence is longer than the one using the hyphenated combination. Remember, though, that word clusters slow down a reader. He might well read and understand the recast version more quickly than the shorter original. Use the words needed to make the meaning clear.

4. When recasting is not feasible, be sure to apply hyphens to achieve clarity. Notice how meaning changes as hyphens shift in the following constructions:

childhood-sex education   childhood sex-education
ugly-letter writer   ugly letter-writer
slow-moving van   slow moving-van

5. The progress from hyphenated to closed word is never sudden. Some people will be writing *praise-worthy* long after others are writing *praiseworthy*. Usually clarity is not affected. Consult a good, current dictionary to check the status of the compound you want to use.

6. Use a hyphen when a spelled-out word modifies a number or a letter.

T-square   6-inch   I-formation   8-cent

7. You are invited to support the growing trend to omit hyphens wherever clarity and ease of reading are not threatened, even when a double vowel results:

antiinflation   reevaluate   cooperate

However, practice varies. If you think *anti-inflation, re-evaluate,* and *co-operate* are easier to read, use hyphens. But always use hyphens to avoid combinations that would fool the eye:

shell-like   re-sort (as opposed to *resort*)

8. Use hyphens between the letters of a spelled-out word.

    b-u-s-i-n-e-s-s

9. Use hyphens to show deleted letters.

    h-ll   d--n   Mr. R-----

10. Hyphenate a phrase used as a single modifier.

    Some people are getting tired of the tell-it-like-it-is fad.

The Dash

1. Make the dash with two strokes of the hyphen key on the type-writer. Do not space before or after the mark.

2. A dash indicates a sudden shift or break in thought.

    It all started thirty years—but why should I tell you that?

    He said he never felt better in his— *[no period]*

3. A dash is sometimes used instead of a comma to indicate an appositive.

    One thing I want from my employees, above all else—loyalty.

    Bring what you can carry—tables, chairs, cooking supplies—in a half-ton pick-up.

4. A dash is sometimes used to show emphasis.

    I'll tell you what to do—sell!

    Save a little money—while you are young—against the troubles of age.

Parentheses

1. Additional information may be enclosed in parentheses—information helpful, but not vital to the sentence.

    I switched from two vintage Buicks (the drip pans alone would lubricate most compacts) to one new Vega.

Since commas, dashes, and parentheses are all used similarly to set off "parenthetical" (incidental) matter, it may be helpful to review or summarize suggestions for their use:

    commas—for closely related matter
    dashes—for emphasis
    parentheses—for less important matter

2. When numbered items are listed in a sentence, use parentheses around item numbers.

> Be sure to have (1) the tools in hand, (2) the water boiling, and (3) the windows open.

3. Use parentheses when repeating a number for accuracy.

> I enclose a check for fourteen dollars and ten cents ($14.10).

4. Use parentheses to enclose an explanatory word not included in the item being recorded.

> It was announced in the *Lancaster* (Pa.) *New Era.*

Brackets

1. The most common use of brackets is in transcribing testimony, hearings, or any long quotation in which the editor or transcriber needs to make an explanation. The explanation may be a simplification of a passage, an editorial comment, an indication, by use of the Latin word *sic*, that an error is recorded exactly as it occurred in the original, the offering of an obviously omitted word or words—whatever may be needed to make clear the passage quoted.

> The head of the defense team said in a recent interview: "The process will, in the final analysis, be a political decision . . . in dealing with the [Judiciary] Committee."
>
> "The president [Kennedy] often spent weekends there."
>
> "Of course he is innocent. [Laughter.] I know he is!"
>
> "They awaited her reply with baited [sic] breath."

2. Use brackets for parentheses within parentheses.

> Two recent books (Simon's *Administrative Behavior*, 3d ed. [1976] and Janis and Mann's *Decision Making* [1977]) pay particular attention to the way decisions are made in business.

Italics (The Underscore)

1. Titles of books, magazines, newspapers, plays, motion pictures, and long poems should be set in italic type (underscored in typescript or handwriting).

> He reads the *Wall Street Journal.*

2. Underscore names of ships, aircraft, and spacecraft and titles of works of art.

> The *Mona Lisa* came over on the SS *America* and went back on the USS *Nautilus*.

3. Legal cases are usually italicized.

> *Brown* v. *Board of Education*

4. Underscore words and phrases that must be emphasized to convey intended meaning.

> Our customers are never *wrong*, Mr. Immelman; stupid, perhaps, and belligerent. But never wrong.

Avoid excessive underscoring for emphasis. Try to choose words that will convey the meaning without additional indicators.

5. Underscore foreign words that have not entered the English language.

> He thought *bête noir* meant he should put his money on the black squares.

6. Underscore a word or expression used as a word or expression.

> The word *Susquehanna* is the prettiest-sounding word in the language.
>
> He inserted *but not always* on the first page and I had to retype the whole dumb thing.

SECTION 33

How to Know When to Capitalize a Word

When people first began to write with an alphabet, they used all capitals, since they had no clear sense of individual words, they wrote an entire utterance without a break. ATYPICALSENTENCEWOULD LOOKLIKETHIS. (If you were to try to record the sounds of a foreign language not known to you, you would do a similar thing.) Of course, the result was rather hard reading.

In time, more and more agreement was achieved about where utterances should be broken, and a sense of what we call *words* developed. Small letters took over most of the job. The large letters were saved for beginnings of units like pages, paragraphs, and sentences. That almost solved the problem. But not quite: there remained the feeling that important people, places, and concepts should have their importance reflected in the word that stood for them on the page. The best way to satisfy this feeling was to use a capital letter at the beginning of such a word. That seems fair enough. The trouble is that at one time or another just about every noun in the language has seemed important to somebody.

The Germans handled this part of the problem nicely. They said that since each noun can be important to somebody sometime, let's capitalize *all* nouns all the time. If we had some sensible arrangement like that for English we could eliminate the question most frequently called from one desk to another across the entire English-speaking world: "Hey, Mabel, do you capitalize. . . ?" Any noun might be the one in question, such as the *belt* in *Bible belt*. The *U.S. Government Printing Office Style Manual* says you don't capitalize, but the logic of that advice is a bit evasive inasmuch as they tell you to capitalize the *belt* in *Corn Belt* and in *Wheat Belt,* all of which refer in a sense to geographical areas.

So practice varies. Fortunately, not much is at stake. If you read *Bible Belt* where you should have read *Bible belt* or *Corn belt* instead of *Corn Belt,* no great harm is done. There is considerable agreement, and we can make the most of that. The following are common rules that you know already, but are listed as a reminder in case you need it.

1. Capitalize the first word of every sentence.

2. Capitalize all proper nouns and many words derived from proper nouns.

   Mary Watts   McAlvey's Fort   German lessons

   But don't capitalize adjectives whose use has taken on a value separate from their earlier connection with a proper noun.

   brazil nut   bowie knife   madras cloth

3. Capitalize names of religious, fraternal, and political organizations.

4. Capitalize titles used with a name or in place of a name.

5. Capitalize names of the days of the week, months of the year, and holidays but not the names of seasons of the year (hardly a fair disposition).

6. Capitalize the first and last words and all important words in between (not articles and prepositions) of titles of books, stories, pamphlets, poems, paintings, movies, plays, and so on.

7. Capitalize the pronoun *I*.

8. Capitalize the first word and each noun in a salutation of a letter, and the first word of a complimentary close.

9. Capitalize points of the compass when they refer to sections of the country but not when they indicate directions.

10. Capitalize the word *Bible*, the names of its books, the names of deities, the names of churches and religious denominations.

For help with the multitude of more troublesome problems, the kind you are most likely to have, consult the University of Chicago Press *Manual of Style*, 12th ed., rev., or *Words into Type*, 3d ed.

SECTION 34

How to Break Words

When possible, avoid breaking a word at the end of a line. When you must break, break between syllables according to pronunciation. Use a hyphen to make the break and put it at the end of the line, never at the beginning of the next line. A dictionary is the best source of information on the syllabic pronunciation of words. Also see section 6, "How to Make Your Letters Attractive and Correct," under the heading *Body of a Letter*. A summary of general rules follows:

1. Don't separate two consonants that are pronounced together.
   bank-er [*not* ban-ker]   hunt-ing [*not* hun-ting]

2. In most cases separate double consonants when they fall between two vowels:
   syl-la-ble   flat-ter   flan-nel
   but not always:
   dwell-er   bill-ing
   Check a dictionary for specific cases.

3. Don't divide words of one syllable.

    helped   treat   store

4. Separate according to pronunciation two vowels sounded separately even though they occur together.

    zo-ol-o-gy   cre-o-sote

5. Don't divide two-syllable words that have only three or four letters.

    ago   era   also   ever   very

6. Don't divide a word so that only one letter is left on a line or only two letters are carried forward.

7. Don't divide words that would confuse the eye if divided.

    women   often   prayer

8. Don't separate dollars from cents, whole numbers from related fractions or decimals, or titles and initials from the names to which they belong.

9. Try not to separate the endings *able* and *ible*.

10. Divide words already hyphenated at the existing hyphen.

11. Don't divide the last word of a letter.

APPENDIX

Additional Forms of Address, Salutation, and Complimentary Close

Since most of the offices in the following list are held traditionally, often exclusively, by men, finding satisfactory forms of address and salutations for women as they fill these positions is an ongoing process. As these jobs are increasingly open to women, new forms will be created. In the meantime, you can follow current practice by substituting an appropriate female title for the one shown in the list. In salutations, use *Ms.*, *Miss*, or *Mrs.* for *Mr.* whenever the male title appears with the surname. Thus, *Dear Mr. Clay* would become *Dear Ms.*, *Miss*, or *Mrs. Clay*. Where *Mr.* appears with a title of office, as in *Dear Mr. Secretary*, you may substitute *Madam* for *Mr.*: *Dear Madam Secretary*. Those who feel uncomfortable with that form can use the title of office with the surname: *Dear Secretary Clay*. Complete addresses obviously cannot be listed here (token addresses for a few federal officials are shown), but a complete local mailing address should, of course, be used.

ADDRESSEE	INSIDE ADDRESS AND ENVELOPE ADDRESS	SALUTATION AND COMPLIMENTARY CLOSE
The Executive Branch		
The president	The President The White House Washington, DC 20500	Dear Mr. President: Respectfully yours,
Assistants to the president	Honorable Adam Clay Assistant to the President The White House	Dear Mr. Clay: Sincerely yours,

The vice president	The Vice President The White House	Dear Mr. Vice President: Sincerely yours,
The cabinet	Honorable Adam Clay Secretary of [dept. name] *or* Attorney General	Dear Mr. Secretary: Sincerely yours, *or* Dear Mr. Attorney General: Sincerely yours,

The Legislature

Senator (in Washington)	Honorable Adam Clay United States Senate Washington, DC 20510	Dear Senator Clay: Sincerely yours,
(away from Washington)	Honorable Adam Clay United States Senator	Dear Senator Clay: Sincerely yours,
Senator-elect	Honorable Adam Clay United States Senator-elect	Dear Mr. Clay: Sincerely yours,
Representative (in Washington)	Honorable Adam Clay House of Representatives Washington, DC 20515	Dear Mr. Clay: Sincerely yours,
(away from Washington)	Honorable Adam Clay Representative in Congress	Dear Mr. Clay: Sincerely yours,
Representative-elect	Honorable Adam Clay Representative in Congress-elect	Dear Mr. Clay: Sincerely yours,

The Judiciary

Chief justice of the United States	Chief Justice of the United States The Supreme Court Washington, DC 20543	Dear Mr. Chief Justice: Sincerely yours,

ADDRESSEE	INSIDE ADDRESS AND ENVELOPE ADDRESS	SALUTATION AND COMPLIMENTARY CLOSE
Associate justice	Mr. Justice Clay The Supreme Court	Dear Mr. Justice: Sincerely yours,
Judge of a court	Honorable Adam Clay Judge of the [name of court; if a U.S. district court, give district]	Dear Judge Clay: Sincerely yours,
Clerk of a court	Mr. Adam Clay Clerk of the [name of court; if a U.S. district court, give district]	Dear Mr. Clay: Sincerely yours,

State and Local Officials

ADDRESSEE	INSIDE ADDRESS AND ENVELOPE ADDRESS	SALUTATION AND COMPLIMENTARY CLOSE
Governor	Honorable Adam Clay Governor of [name of state]	Dear Governor Clay: Sincerely yours,
Lieutenant governor	Honorable Adam Clay Lieutenant Governor of [name of state]	Dear Mr. Clay: Sincerely yours,
Secretary of state	Honorable Adam Clay Secretary of State of [name of state]	Dear Mr. Secretary: Sincerely yours,
Chief justice of a state supreme court	Honorable Adam Clay Chief Justice Supreme Court of the State of [name of state]	Dear Mr. Chief Justice: Sincerely yours,
State attorney general	Honorable Adam Clay Attorney General State of [name of state]	Dear Mr. Attorney General: Sincerely yours,
Judge	Honorable Adam Clay	Dear Judge Clay: Sincerely yours,

State treasurer, auditor, or comptroller	Honorable Adam Clay State Treasurer [Auditor, Comptroller] State of [name of state]	Dear Mr. Clay: Sincerely yours,
State senator	Honorable Adam Clay [name of state] Senate	Dear Senator Clay: Sincerely yours,
State representative, assemblyman, or delegate	Honorable Adam Clay [name of state, House of Representatives, House of Delegates, or Assembly]	Dear Mr. Clay: Sincerely yours,
Mayor	Honorable Adam Clay Mayor of [name of city]	Dear Mayor Clay: Sincerely yours,
President of a board of commissioners	Honorable Adam Clay President, Board of Commissioners of [name of city]	Dear Mr. Clay: Sincerely yours,
Religious Leaders		
Protestant minister, pastor, or rector (with a doctor's degree)	The Reverend Adam Clay, [initials of degree] [title, name of church]	Dear Dr. Clay: Sincerely yours,
(without a doctor's degree)	The Reverend Adam Clay	Dear Mr. Clay: Sincerely yours,
Rabbi (with a doctor's degree)	Rabbi Adam Clay, [initials of degree]	Dear Dr. Clay: Dear Rabbi Clay: [1] Sincerely yours,
(without a doctor's degree)	Rabbi Adam Clay	Dear Rabbi Clay: Sincerely yours,
Catholic cardinal	His Eminence Adam Cardinal Clay Archbishop of [name of diocese]	Your Eminence: Dear Cardinal Clay: Sincerely yours,

1. When two salutations are given, the first is the more formal. Increasingly, American practice is to use the less formal.

ADDRESSEE	INSIDE ADDRESS AND ENVELOPE ADDRESS	SALUTATION AND COMPLIMENTARY CLOSE
Catholic archbishop	The Most Reverend Adam Clay Archbishop of [name of diocese]	Your Excellency: Dear Archbishop Clay: Sincerely yours,
Catholic bishop	The Most Reverend Adam Clay Bishop of [name of diocese]	Your Excellency: Dear Bishop Clay: Sincerely yours,
Catholic monsignor (higher rank)	The Right Reverend Monsignor Adam Clay	Right Reverend Monsignor: Dear Monsignor Clay: Sincerely yours,
(papal chamberlain)	The Very Reverend Monsignor Adam Clay	Very Reverend Monsignor: Dear Monsignor Clay: Sincerely yours,
Catholic priest	The Reverend Adam Clay, [initials of order, or degree, if used]	Reverend Father: Dear Father Clay: Sincerely yours,
Women of religious communities (for a mother superior who uses a religious name)	Mother Mary Margaret, [initials of order, if used] [title, name of institution]	Dear Mother Mary Margaret: Sincerely yours,
(for a mother superior who uses her last name)	Mother Mary Margaret Clay	Dear Mother Mary Margaret: Sincerely yours,
(for a director who prefers Sister and who uses a religious name)	Sister Mary Margaret, [initials of order, if used] [title, name of institution]	Dear Sister Mary Margaret: Sincerely yours,

(for a director who prefers *Sister* and who uses her given name)	Sister Amy Clay	Dear Sister Amy: Sincerely yours,
(for a sister who uses a religious name)	Sister Mary Margaret, [initials of order, if used]	Dear Sister Mary Margaret: Sincerely yours,
(for a sister who uses her given name)	Sister Amy Clay	Dear Sister Amy: Sincerely yours,
Mormon bishop	Mr. Adam Clay Church of Jesus Christ of Latter Day Saints	Sir: Dear Mr. Clay: Sincerely yours,
Protestant Episcopal bishop	The Right Reverend Adam Clay Bishop of [name of city]	Right Reverend Sir: Dear Bishop Clay: Sincerely yours,
Protestant Episcopal dean	The Very Reverend Adam Clay Dean of [name of church]	Very Reverend Sir: Dear Dean Clay: Sincerely yours,
Methodist bishop	The Reverend Adam Clay Methodist Bishop	Reverend Sir: My dear Bishop: Sincerely yours,
Chaplain	Chaplain Adam Clay	Dear Chaplain Clay: Sincerely yours,
Academic Officials		
President of a college or university (with a doctor's degree)	Adam Clay, [initials of degree] President, [name of institution]	Dear Dr. Clay: Sincerely yours,
(without a doctor's degree)	Mr. Adam Clay President, [name of institution]	Dear Mr. Clay: Sincerely yours,

ADDRESSEE	INSIDE ADDRESS AND ENVELOPE ADDRESS	SALUTATION AND COMPLIMENTARY CLOSE
Dean of a school (with a doctor's degree)	Adam Clay, [initials of degree] Dean, [name of school] [name of institution]	Dear Dr. Clay: Sincerely yours,
(without a doctor's degree)	Dean Adam Clay [name of school]	Dear Dean Clay: Sincerely yours,

INDEX

A

Abbreviations
  in addresses, 35
  in letter headings, 34
  in military titles, 39–40
  in report text, 79
  in titles, 37–38
  of states, territories, 34
  for ZIP codes, 35
Abstract, 103, 105; *see also* Synopsis
Academic officials, addressing, 229
Accepting a job, letter, 28–29
Acknowledgments, in reports, 70
Active voice, 165
Address, forms of, 224–30
Address of writer; *see* Heading, 34–36
Almanacs, 133
Analysis, 96–97
And, beginning sentence with, 152
Anecdote, definition by, 94–95
Antecedent of pronoun, 163
Apostrophe, 214–16
Appendix, 81–82
Application blank, for job, 26–27
Attention line, 47
Authorization letter, 67

B

Background, in reports, 77–78
Basis of classification, 96
Bibliography, how to prepare, 80–81, 148
Block style, 50, 51
Body
  of letter, 42–43
  of report, 79

Brackets, 219
Breaking words, 222–23
Business magazine indexes, 135–36
Business operating guides, 126–27
But, beginning sentence with, 152

C

Capitalization, 220–22
  in salutation, 41
Captions, 75
Carbon copies, 48
Catchall words, 170
Charts
  how to list, 75
  how to use, 86–90
Choppy sentences, 156
Citing sources, 80–81, 146–51
Clarity, 3–5, 138–39
Classification, 96–97
Clichés, 173–75
Collection letter, 6, 19
Colloquialism, 186
Colon, 41, 91, 213–14
Comma, 41, 208–12
Comparison, 94
Completeness, 137
Complimentary close, 43–47, 224–29
Conciseness, 4–5, 137
Conclusions
  in full-dress report, 79–80
  how to state, 97–99
  position in report, 64–65
  in transmittal letter, 71
Connotation, 151, 170
Contents, table of, 73–75
Contrast, 94
Coordination, 156–57

Government officials, addressing, 224–27
Government periodicals, 132–33
Government publications, 136–37
Graphics, 86–91
Gunning fog index, 139

H

Heading, letter, 34–36
Headings, in reports, 83–86
History, in reports, 77–78
Hyphen, 216–18

I

Identifying initials in letters, 48
Illustration, definition by, 94–95
Illustrations
  how to list, 75
  how to use, 86–91
Informal level in writing, 169
Information services, 134
Inside address, 36–40
Introduction, 76–79, 92–93
Invented words, 169
Italics, 219–20

J

Jargon, 195; see also Catchall words
Job application blank, 26–27
Job application letters, 6, 19–30
  accepting job, 28–29
  cover letter 20–26
  follow-up, 27–28
  points to remember, 29–30

refusing job, 29
résumé, 20–22
Job application rejections, 6, 12

L

Lay, lie, 196
Leave, let, 196
Letter
  analysis of, 3–6
  body of, 42–43
  categories of, 5–6
  definition of, 3
  formats, 50–52
  margins, 31
  paper, 30–31
  parts of, 31–49
  placement scale, 32
  spacing, 31, 33
Letters, types of
  accepting job, 28–29
  authorization, 67
  bad-news, 5–6, 10–15
  collection, 6, 19
  cover, job application, 20–26
  credit refusal, 12–13
  follow-up, job application, 27–28
  good-news, 6–10
  goodwill, 9–10
  job application rejection, 6, 12
  "no," 5–6, 10–15
  persuasive request, 6, 15–18
  "please do something," 5–6, 15–19
  recommendation, 122
  refusal, 6, 12, 13–15
  refusing job, 29
  request, 15–19
  sales, 6, 18
  transmittal, 70, 72
  "yes," 5–10
Level of usage, 168–69

P2